Performance Kayaking

Stephen B. U'Ren

Stackpole Books

Published by
STACKPOLE BOOKS
Cameron and Kelker Streets
P.O. Box 1831
Harrisburg, PA 17105

Printed in the United States of America

10 9 8 7 6 5

First Edition

Photo credits: cover, chapters 1–6, 8–9—George I. Thomas;
            chapter 7—Ed Michael
Illustrated by Andrea K. U'Ren

Cover design by Tracy Patterson

Library of Congress Cataloging-in-Publication Data

U'Ren, Stephen B.
    Performance kayaking / Stephen B. U'Ren.—1st ed.
        p. cm.
    Includes bibliographical references.
    ISBN 0-8117-2299-6
    1. Kayaking. I. Title.
GV783.U74 1990
    797.1'22—dc20   89-38088
                                                    CIP

Contents

Acknowledgments   v

Introduction   vi

An Important Note to Readers   viii

ONE   Getting Going   1

Choosing a boat, outfitting your
boat, trimming your boat, caring
for your boat, boating gear, clothing, safety gear, tips for those who
wear glasses and contact lenses

TWO   Boating Basics   15

Holding your paddle, types of
strokes, posture, balance, blade
angle

THREE   Propulsion and
           Turning Strokes   23

The forward stroke, the reverse
stroke, the sweep, the reverse
sweep, the rudder, the draw, the
duffek, combination strokes

FOUR   Recovery Strokes
           and Maneuvers   47

The hip snap, low and high braces,
the sweeping brace, the sweep roll,
the hip-snap roll, the extended paddle roll, the hands roll, the back roll,
whitewater rolling strategies

FIVE   **Reading White Water**   **65**

Whitewater morphology, waves, channels, converging currents, obstacles, logs and strainers, undercuts and potholes, boils, pillows, eddies, eddylines, rooster tails, walls, holes, waterfalls, river rating

SIX   **Whitewater Maneuvers**   **87**

The elements of safety, paddling in waves, ferries, back ferries, eddy turns, peel-outs, S turns

SEVEN   **Play Paddling**   **121**

Wave surfing, enders, hole riding, whitewater rodeo

EIGHT   **The Next Step**   **143**

Running rapids, using eddies and holes, rebounding off pillows and stoppers, rock gardens, running waterfalls, paddling downstream through an eddy, paddling upstream, playing games, pivot turns and stern squirts, paddling different types of white water

NINE   **Slalom Racing**   **169**

Slalom rules, slalom basics, downstream gates in waves, offsets, upstream gates, S turns, reverses, ferries between gates, eddies between gates, a downstream in an eddy, at the races

Suggested Reading and Viewing   184

Acknowledgments

Many people considerably improved the quality of *Performance Kayaking* by offering their suggestions and comments. Deep thanks go to my father Richard U'Ren, my mother Marjorie Burns, Doris Lopez, Herbert Bowman, Tom Linde, Dave Harrison, and Susan Mahoney. Many, many thanks go to George Thomas, who not only shot excellent photos under trying conditions, but also doubled as friend and adviser. Leslie Reid's astute comments and useful suggestions were immensely valuable. Much appreciation also goes to my sister, Andrea U'Ren, for her entertaining and accurate illustrations in spite of a less-than-complete paddling background.

The chapter on play paddling benefited from Doug Ammons's editorial help.

Thanks also to Nimbus, distributors of Quality Kayaks International's Alpha kayak; Patagonia; Wildwasser Sports U.S.A., distributors of Prijon, Schlegel, and Yak products; Native paddles; Northwest Design Works, Inc., makers of Werner paddles; and Northwest River Supply, distributors of Wildwater helmets and other river gear.

Introduction

There's nothing quite like the feeling of zipping around on a whitewater river, flying over drops into deep pools, cutting back and forth on fast surf-waves, and frolicking like an otter in play spots. There are lots of reasons to whitewater kayak, but probably the best one is that it's a lot of fun. Kayaking allows you to escape the day-to-day routine, to meet people, to experience thrills, to face technical challenges, and simply to relax in the outdoors. Feeling your body and mind work and play with the river is spiritually refreshing. Kayaking makes you feel vibrant; it both nourishes the body and stimulates the mind. Whatever your reasons and rewards, you need to know how to read water and maneuver your boat. And you have more fun when you are more proficient.

If you're a beginner, you'll learn the essential whitewater skills from this book. And if you already kayak a little or a lot, you'll find this book helpful for fine-tuning your whitewater technique and strategy. The term *performance* is not meant to imply that this book is exclusively for those interested in competition. Whatever your aspirations, *Performance Kayaking* can improve your paddling skills.

Performance Kayaking is written in a progressive format: the book starts off with the fundamentals and then builds on them. As much as possible, this approach is also taken within individual chapters. But *Performance Kayaking's* main strength is that much of it has been written with both novices and advanced paddlers in mind. I hope that advanced paddlers will read the more fundamental sections with the same intensity that they read the advanced sections. Often, it's boaters who have been paddling for a long time who need the most work on their technique. Bad habits become ingrained and reinforced through years of incorrect paddling. The section on the often underrated forward stroke, for instance, is rich in information and provides a wealth of particulars for paddlers who want to learn the small details that will ultimately make a profound difference in their whitewater effectiveness. *Performance Kayaking* is, then, somewhat like a child's oversized shirt—paddlers can grow into the book and keep learning from it as their skills improve.

Given the emphasis on technique, there's relatively little space for comprehensive discussion of certain other aspects of river kayaking—accessory gear, for instance. The nuances of river rescue techniques are also not discussed to the extent they deserve. This is not meant to de-emphasize these important topics; they are simply not within the scope of this book.

Chapter Seven, Play Paddling, is written by Bob McDougall. Bob is a premier play paddler and rodeo champion and has made numerous first descents on rivers around the world. He is eminently qualified to write about the nuances of surfing, endering, and hole playing. His laid-back and groovy style has a different tone from the rest of the text, but it adds nice contrast and balance. In short, Bob is a fun-hog and will convert you into one, too.

Since this book is dedicated to the teaching of technique and finesse, I hope that it will help dispel the chauvinistic notion that it takes primarily muscles to maneuver a boat on a river. Many paddlers, especially men, try to beat the river into submission. Strength and skill are both necessary, but since the river will always be stronger, the development of finesse is the more rewarding and valuable characteristic to possess.

Performance Kayaking is about how to paddle a kayak on a river safely and elegantly. The goal is to teach paddlers not how to simply survive a river, but how to play and work *with* it. All the book's themes center on one premise: with good river technique comes freedom . . . and with freedom comes pleasure.

Enjoy.

S.B.U.

An Important Note to Readers

Performance Kayaking describes how to whitewater kayak, but the publisher and author cannot be responsible for your safety. There's obviously no way that any book can substitute for actual river experience in this potentially dangerous sport. As all athletes know, you can't get good at something just by reading about it. At some point, you're going to have to get out on the water and practice. Read this book, but also join a clinic, club, or group of experienced paddlers. This is the most effective way to learn kayaking skills. Your challenge is to synthesize technical information with intuition and the feeling for the water that is difficult to communicate, but absolutely essential.

Performance Kayaking does require the reader to have a minimal level of knowledge. It assumes, for example, that the reader knows, or will shortly know (through a class or clinic), how to get into a boat and what a sprayskirt is. The very basic details that aren't developed here can be gathered by visiting your nearest outfitter or by talking to other boaters. For additional information, see *Suggested Reading and Viewing* at the end of the book.

ONE

Getting Going

EVERY ASPECT OF OUTFITTING IS ESSENTIAL to perform-ance kayaking. To begin whitewater kayaking, you first need a boat and the necessary paddling gear. Well-made, long-lasting equipment is always worth the in-vestment. Since your boat is the most expensive piece of equipment, you'll want to select a design that fits the kind of boating you want to do.

Choosing a Boat

Every year, more and more kayak designs come onto the market. This makes choosing a boat harder than in years past, when only a few designs were available. This is true for glass as well as for plastic designs (the term *glass* refers to any boat made with resin and either fiberglass or a synthetic, such as Kevlar or graphite).

There are always trade-offs inherent in any design. No one boat does every river maneuver perfectly; every boat has its strengths and weaknesses. If you have the luxury of owning two or more boats, you can change boats the way golfers change clubs, depending on the water level or your mood. There are six main cate-gories in whitewater kayaking: river running, touring, play boating, slalom racing, downriver racing, and squirt boating. Some boats are designed to excel in

BOAT DESIGNS

ROCKERED HULL

UNROCKERED HULL

A rockered boat has a convex hull from bow to stern while an unrockered boat doesn't. Highly rockered boats spin more easily than those with less rocker. Boats with little rocker, however, paddle in a straight line more easily than rockered ones.

only one of these specialized fields, but most handle adequately in several.

RIVER RUNNING. You can run a river in just about anything, but some boats are particularly suited to certain rivers, depending on water volume, grade, and so on. To a large extent, however, you can adapt your technique to compensate for a particular quality your boat may lack. Most river kayaks are plastic because of plastic's resiliency, but there are numerous glass boats that are quite durable. Plastic boats require little maintenance in comparison with glass boats and are thus the choice of most boaters.

For water suited to the average paddler almost any whitewater boat will do. If you're going to be paddling big, tumultuous water, you may want a bigger boat with enough volume to keep it on the surface. A boat that has additional width and a fairly flat bottom gives extra stability. Every whitewater kayak also has a certain amount of rocker, the degree to which the ends are above the middle of the boat; the greater the rocker, the easier a boat will spin. A minor trade-off is that a highly rockered boat can sometimes be difficult to keep on an intended line; white water can spin it about with relative ease.

For small, steep, and technical river runs, a short boat with relatively large volume is best. The short length lets the boat spin quickly and presents less boat surface in rock-choked rivers. The high volume keeps the boat buoyant, and the bow will pop right up to the surface after you've run a drop instead of "penciling" deep into the water.

TOURING. Touring kayaks are designed primarily for extended camping trips on easy white water. They're relatively long, wide, and big (high-volume), to accommodate the storage of gear. Since their main purpose is to move efficiently in easy white water, they tend to have very little bow-to-stern rocker, which makes them hard to turn. Since they're long (longer than the standard of a 13-foot slalom boat), they're easy to paddle in a straight line. Touring boats also tend to be stable because of their substantial width.

PLAY PADDLING. Play paddling is the art of river trickery using holes, waves, and pour-overs. Whitewater rodeos are competitions in which paddlers vie for the most original and technically precise stunts. These tricks include spinning in holes, endering (getting shot out of the water on-end), and wave surfing. Generally, boats 12 feet or shorter are the best for play paddling; they spin more quickly than longer boats and fit snugly into holes and short, steep waves. A decent play boat has a lot of rocker in its hull, making it easy to spin. Also, good play boats have very soft and rounded chines, or rails, where their sides meet their bottoms; this makes them relatively forgiving and smooth-handling.

RACING. There are two types of whitewater racing: slalom and downriver. Slalom kayaks are low-volume in order to turn quickly and sneak under slalom poles. They have quite a bit of rocker, which helps their turning ability and are also long (slightly over 13 feet), which makes them fairly fast when paddled in a straight line. In addition, slalom boats usually have hard chines and sharp edges, which makes them very responsive in white water but also somewhat unstable, at least starting out. Slalom designs are fast, responsive, and great fun to paddle except on tremendously big or steep water.

Downriver boats are designed for speed on white water. Typically, DR boats (as they're called) race from point A to point B on a five-mile or so stretch of Class III white water. Compared with slalom boats, they're high-volumed (to shed the water from waves) and long (about 15 feet) for increased straight-ahead speed. Their rounded narrow hulls make them fast but tippy. They have essentially no rocker, which makes them unwieldy to turn but also fast.

SQUIRT BOATING. Squirt boating has literally opened up a new dimension to river paddling. Instead of using only the two-dimensional surface currents that most boats are limited to, these extremely low-volume edgy boats use subsurface currents as well as visible surface currents to perform their tricks. Thus,

BOAT DESIGNS

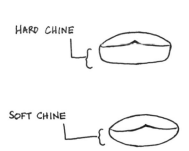

HARD CHINE

SOFT CHINE

Chine is the amount of sharpness between a boat's side and bottom. A boat's chine, or rail, affects its stability and responsiveness. Play boats tend to be soft-chined; slalom boats usually have harder chine.

three-dimensional boating is possible. Stunts include stern or bow squirts, putting the boat vertical on either end; cartwheels, alternating bow and stern squirts; splatters, intentional vertical pins on rocks; and mystery moves, spinning the boat while upright but underwater, head and all.

Expert squirters say that squirt boats are great in both big and small water, but these kayaks are probably best for the average paddler in easy to intermediate water because of their tippiness. As with any boat, you can tackle harder water as your skills increase. Squirt boats are also great during low-water season because you can still do many squirt maneuvers on slow, easy water.

Outfitting Your Boat

A snug fit in the boat is crucial to good paddling technique. Not having a solid, comfortable fit in your kayak is just like wearing a 10D shoe on a 9B foot. Wear your kayak; don't just sit in it. It's no fun to fall out of your boat every time you tip over, or to feel awkward and unstable on the river because your outfitting is marginal. Your body should make solid contact with your boat at four spots: feet, knees, hips, and back. Your overall fit should be slightly loose for comfort's sake, with just enough margin that merely tensing your feet and thighs causes you and the boat to become one.

FOOT BRACING. Your feet need to be placed firmly against the foot braces so that you have good control of your boat. You want your foot bracing tight so that your knees are pressed up into the knee braces and your back is pressed against the backstrap or butt-pad. If your feet fall asleep, your foot braces are too tight (too far toward the cockpit), but snugness is important; experiment to find that happy medium. If you're new to kayaking, your legs might fall asleep fairly easily, even with what will later seem a loose fit. After some time, your legs will adjust and stretch out; at that time you'll want to tighten the foot braces.

Position your feet so that your heels are close together, with toes turned out and the whole foot fairly flat and at about a 90-degree angle to your ankles. It's best to have the balls of your feet in contact with the foot braces.

Boat outfitting. Notice the padded backstrap as well as the hip pads on both sides of the seat. Knee pads help keep knees and thighs in place for stability and control. The lengthwise bar under the seat gives the hull rigidity, an important consideration for both safety and performance.

Sometimes the front support pillar, or wall, in a stock boat is so thick that it's impossible to get your feet and ankles in the correct position. Your feet end up pointed forward, ballerina style, and crammed between the pillar and the side. Not only is this painful, it doesn't give you good boat control. This is especially a problem in low-volume boats for those who happen to have big feet. You can, however, alleviate this problem by cutting a hole in the wall with a bread knife or coping saw—a space just big enough to allow your heels to nestle together without compromising the structural integrity of the wall.

There's a wide assortment of commercially available foot braces, and nearly all are adjustable. some are pegs that stick out from the side and are just big enough for the balls of your feet, others are bars that span the width of the boat, still others are solid blocks of foam that brace your whole foot rather than just the ball of your foot. The last is the most comfortable option. The only problem with bars and blocks is that it's impossible to stretch your feet out past them. Foot braces that stick out from each side, but are not connected to one another in the midline of the boat, allow you to stretch your feet and legs when they cramp.

You can inexpensively resin a fiberglass or wooden dowel from side to side in a glass boat. Although not adjustable, this type of foot peg provides a good individual fit.

Nonetheless, adjustable foot braces are the best option, since they allow a loose fit for longer trips on easy water and a firm fit for tough stretches of white water. Plus, you can trade boats with other paddlers. Foot braces that are adjustable while you're sitting in the boat are especially convenient as you don't need to get in and out of the boat to get that perfect fit. Beware of getting sand or dirt in the adjustment mechanism; your previously adjustable foot braces could become jammed. This is especially frustrating if you've just lent your boat to Magic Johnson or Larry Bird. Unjam them with persistent wiggling and cajoling.

KNEE AND THIGH BRACING. Knees and hips are responsible for most of a kayaker's balancing and leaning. The wider you can get your knees, the better your side-to-side balancing will be. Try sitting on the floor with your legs straight out; then rock from side to side. Now try it with your feet drawn up and your knees out to each side. It's easy to tell which position is more stable.

Some stock boats on the market tend to force the knees inward more than is desirable, and although they afford a good leg position for a powerful forward stroke, they detract from the ability to lean and balance the boat effectively. It's easy to fix this by padding your knee braces with some type of closed-cell foam, such as Ensolite or form-fitted Minicell. Padding has two advantages: by effectively lowering the deck, it allows you to spread your knees farther apart and still be braced in firmly, and if you build up the edge toward the cockpit rim, you'll actually get more surface area to brace against. Knee padding also lets you grip hard with your knees and thighs without feeling as though your kneecaps are being squashed against a brick wall.

Knee braces that are big enough to make contact with both knees and thighs give maximum control. Some paddlers even install form-fitted foam blocks to the outside of the knee and thigh position so that their legs won't move inward or outward when maneuvering. This setup gives the firmest fit. Whatever sort of knee bracing you decide on, be sure you can easily slide in and out of your boat.

HIP PADDING. The point of contact between boat and hips is important because it's the first place force reaches the boat as it moves through the paddle, body, and into the seat. It's also an important balance point and is necessary for proper recovery technique, lest you fall out of the boat when you flip. Without a firm connection between your hips and the seat, you can do any number of upper body gyrations but never effectively transfer the energy to your boat. Sliding around in the seat decreases your ability to react immediately to river conditions. Gluing some Minicell or Ensolite foam padding on your seat to fill in those extra spaces will make all the difference. Hip pads that are thicker on both their upper and their stern ends are particularly useful in helping to secure you in the boat. This shape keeps you from sliding around while still allowing your knees to spread for optimal balancing.

BACK SUPPORT. The back is the most commonly neglected point of contact with the boat. Most paddlers' backbands aren't tight enough, and some people even paddle in a state of ignorant bliss without any type of back support. A backstrap fulfills two functions: it helps transfer energy from every stroke to the boat and it helps keep you upright—critical to the proper placement of a stroke. In this second capacity, it keeps you from leaning on the back deck, which is a sure sign of a tired or lazy paddler. Also, it helps prevent back pain. Your back support should be tight enough to maintain good posture, but not so tight that it causes you to bend forward or causes your legs to fall asleep. It needs to be placed so that it supports the small of your back, and adjusted so that you can get in and out of the boat with ease.

Back support comes in a variety of forms, but in plastic boats the most common is an extended rear foam pillar. Typically, this provides insufficient support. However, if the pillar is wide, comes up high on your back, and is tailored to your body, the support will be fine. A backstrap is the best option to use because it spreads the support over the horizontal arc of your lower back. Most commercially available straps are adjustable and can be bolted into either plastic or fiberglass seats. A decent homemade version can be made using 2- to 3-inch webbing or by padding a strip of stiff, but flexible, plastic with neoprene or Ensolite.

Trimming Your Boat

Your boat needs to be balanced front to back so that when you sit in it on still water, each end is the same height above the waterline. How the boat is balanced when it sits on the water is called its trim. Uneven trim makes the boat difficult to maneuver. All boats spin best around their midpoint—the middle spot that is deepest in the water. Moving the deepest point away from the geometrical midpoint compromises any boat's spinning ability. Specifically, extreme bow heaviness can cause the boat to pearl, or nose under, as well as make it hard to turn. Since even well-trimmed boats plane up (the bow rises and the stern sinks) somewhat when paddled forward, a boat with stern-heavy trim will be particularly sluggish when paddled straight ahead.

To check your trim, have a friend on shore observe the relative positions of bow and stern. Then adjust your seat accordingly and get back out on the water for a recheck. Most stock boats are already pretty well balanced, but since everyone's body is different, it's not a bad idea to check and adjust if you have the option of an adjustable seat. Err on the side of slight bow heaviness if it's a close call.

Caring For Your Boat

Whatever boat you have, keep it in good shape so that it performs the way it was designed to and retains its resale value as well. A boat whose hull gets thin, soft, and mushy will deform or "oilcan" when you paddle it. Oilcanning occurs when an old hull reverberates as water pushes against it; you can hear a rumbling. A deformed or oilcanning hull keeps the boat from moving and turning responsively, and this, in turn, limits what you can do with the boat.

With time, all boats get thinner and softer because of the constant pounding and abrasion. Hulls also deform slightly, but you hasten the process by storing a boat on its bottom and tying it too tightly to a roof rack. To maximize your boat's longevity, store it on its side or suspended from ropes—either by its grab loops or cradled by straps or ropes. To transport your kayak, use hull-shaped cradles on your roof rack. Avoid storing or leaving your boat (especially if it's plastic) in the hot sun for extended periods; high heat can actually melt your boat. Ultraviolet rays weaken most chemical bonds and may cause your boat's color to fade.

Boating Gear

PADDLES. Every halfway-decent whitewater kayak paddle nowadays has curved blades for a better bite in the water than a flat blade. Typically, curved blades are also offset, or feathered, from each other at an angle of 75 to 90 degrees.

There are many brands of paddles made from different materials, but any well-constructed paddle weighing between 2 and 2½ pounds should be strong enough for normal use. Lighter paddles are easier to use, but paddles much below 2 pounds may not hold up in a crunch. Any paddle weighing close to 3 pounds will cause you to tire quickly.

The stiffer the paddle, the more efficient your stroke. A stiff paddle transfers your force immediately to the water. A flexible paddle leads to a loss of energy.

It's important to get the correct paddle length. The optimal length depends on your height, the length of your arms, and your preferred style of paddling. Add a few centimeters for some extra support and leverage in big water. If you're slalom racing, subtract a couple of centimeters to keep from hitting the poles. If your arms are exceptionally long, you may want to figure on the long end.

Your Height	Paddle Length
5'3"	196–200 cm
5'5"	198–202 cm
5'7"	200–204 cm
5'9"	202–206 cm
5'11"	204–208 cm
6'1"	206–210 cm
6'3"	208–212 cm

GETTING A TIGHT GRIP. Finally, you need a solid grip on the shaft so that your hands don't unintentionally slide while holding the paddle—an aquatic version of a greased pig contest. It's a nasty surprise to suddenly find both hands together, at the throat of one blade, at a crucial moment in the middle of a big drop.

Lightly sanding the gripping area of the shaft with some very fine sandpaper or steel wool will help the grip. If you're on the river, some wet sand or dirt will also do the job.

A more effective and permanent way to maintain a great grip is to glue some thin rubber to the shaft with contact cement. A bicycle inner tube works well for this. You really need it only where the control hand grips; too much friction on the noncontrol hand may cause blisters.

SPRAYSKIRTS. The fit of your sprayskirt, both around your waist and around the cockpit rim, is important to your paddling enjoyment and safety. It's no fun to have your skirt pop off halfway through a rapid. A good skirt provides a virtually watertight seal. The skirt should be flat and tight when it's on the cockpit rim (also called a cauling or coaming) to prevent water from pooling. Neoprene skirts are far superior to nylon ones in their fit and sealing ability. Neoprene will, to a small extent, stretch when wet. The waist fit should be snug but not inhibit breathing. Factor in the extra thickness that cold weather garb will add to your girth when you're deciding what size to purchase.

To determine the correct tension of the skirt around the cockpit rim, put the skirt on your empty boat and lift up by grabbing the middle of the skirt with both hands. Depending on the weight of the boat, the skirt should stay connected to the boat for a brief time (about three seconds assuming a boat weight of 35 pounds). If it pops right off, it's too loose. If it clings like a leech, it's too tight and you may have problems getting out in an emergency.

LIFE JACKETS. There are a number of good, Coast Guard–approved life jackets, or Personal Flotation Devices (PFDs), on the market. They come in all sorts of designs and thicknesses. Life jackets fulfill a dual function: when you're swimming through a rapid, they help keep you afloat, and when you're upside-down in your boat, they offer back and shoulder protection from subsurface hazards. In general, the higher the buoyancy rating of the jacket, the better.

The only drawback with a really big life jacket is its bulkiness. This can be a technical limitation in a couple of paddling fields. Slalom racers, for example, use only a minimally padded (but still approved) life jacket to keep from hitting the gates, and squirt boaters avoid bulky jackets because many squirt maneuvers require minimal flotation—and intentional full-body submersion. But most boaters should start off with a big PFD. As you get better, you can use the less restrictive ones. But if you start running difficult water, return to a high-flotation jacket.

Wear a jacket that fits. Most jackets are to some extent adjustable, with straps on each side. Tighten these straps so that your PFD won't slide around or ride up over your face should you swim. To check the fit, stretch your arms over your head and have a friend grab the jacket's shoulders and try to pull it off over your head. A good fit will make this difficult.

HELMETS. It can be argued that your helmet is the single most important piece of safety equipment. As with life jackets, there are oodles of helmets on the market. Although a snug fit is absolutely necessary for adequate protection, you can get a headache if your helmet is too tight. Some helmets are adjustable, but most come in small, medium, and large sizes. If your helmet is somewhat loose and nonadjustable, glue in some foam to tighten the fit. A well-fitting helmet shouldn't jiggle when you shake your head.

The safest helmets are designed somewhat like bicycle helmets and are completely lined with foam. Most helmets that cover your ears will provide excellent protection.

Clothing

An endless topic. The bottom line: dress appropriately. Avoid over- or under-dressing for the anticipated temperature. You want neither heatstroke nor hypothermia. Because getting cold, or hypothermic, is the most common river danger, it's better to err on the side of warmth, but try not to overdo it. If it's 90 degrees out and the water temperature is 75, don't wear your drysuit with all the insulating trimmings. You'll not only stew in your own juices and get sleepy and lazy from the heat, you'll also lose your friends when you release those simmered bodily vapors into the environment. If you're unsure how many layers of clothes to wear, bring some extra clothes in a drybag and put them on if the need arises. Finally, make sure your padding clothes fit well but don't restrict movement.

DRYSUITS. In cold weather a drysuit over some insulating layers will keep you warmer than any other combination. Drysuits come in one-piece and two-piece styles. Their rubber gaskets and waterproof zippers keep you essentially dry, even when rolling. Both styles are equally waterproof, but the two-piece suits give you the option of wearing just the top as a paddle jacket when the temperature is too warm to justify a full drysuit.

INSULATION. Any of the modern synthetics made from polyester or polypropylene are good for keeping you warm while paddling. Pile fabrics are comfortable and warm. Wool is always a fine insulator, though it doesn't dry as quickly as synthetic fibers. Layering your clothes is a good idea; you can put on layers or take them off as needed.

PADDLE JACKETS. Almost every paddle jacket on the market is made of nylon. Variations in quality are primarily a result of different types of waterproof coating on the inside of the jacket. Some of the more inexpensive paddle jackets have a urethane coating that peels off after a few years, turning the paddle jacket into something more like a spaghetti colander than a water-shedder. High-quality coatings will last for years.

Wear a paddle jacket that fits. It's especially important to have some range of motion when your arms are extended so that you don't feel bound up when stroking. Your jacket should go over your sprayskirt and be cinched fairly tightly to keep water out.

You can also purchase a drytop by itself to use as a paddling jacket. A drytop is drier than a paddle jacket but won't keep you as warm as a drysuit. Since your legs are insulated somewhat by the boat, if you're not going to swim, a drytop is a good option over the full suit when conditions are cold, but not frigid.

WETSUITS. Farmer John wetsuits are like wetsuit overalls. Used in combination with an external paddle jacket, they provide a fine insulating system. Avoid wetsuit jackets, though; the arms are too restrictive for kayaking. They'll exhaust you by making you feel as though you've got huge, stiff, rubber bands on each arm, which is indeed the case. Be sure to get a suit that's equal to or thinner than 3/8 inch; otherwise you'll find your torso movement restricted.

Wetsuit booties with tread are good. They make walking over river rocks easy and keep your feet warm.

Safety Gear

BOAT FLOTATION. First off, make sure your boat has plenty of flotation in it. A combination of support pillars and inflatable float bags will keep your boat from sinking should you swamp it. And if you swim out of your boat, a kayak filled with float bags is easier to tow to shore than one filled with water. Some float bags double as gear storage sacks.

THROW ROPES AND SAFETY GEAR. A throw rope is an important item of safety gear. Throw ropes are thrown by someone on the bank to a swimmer; the thrower then braces himself and pendulums the swimmer downstream into shore. Ropes are also invaluable for unpinning boats from rocks. If your group has only one throw rope, the best boater should carry it.

Carabiners and prussik slings are vital for many river rescue operations.

FIRST-AID KITS. A first-aid kit is always good to have along. Keep it dry and stocked with basic first-aid materials. A kit can be bought at any recreation store or assembled on your own.

DRYBAGS. A drybag to store lunch, a first-aid kit, and extra clothing is nice to have along. Be sure to clip it to the inside of the boat so that it doesn't float free if you swim.

Tips for Those Who Wear Glasses and Contact Lenses

Depending on the type of helmet you have, your glasses may or may not fit well. If your helmet feels uncomfortably tight, simply cut channels in the foam lining to accommodate the stems of your glasses.

Although it's always important for contact lens wearers to keep their eyes closed while underwater, most people who lose contacts on the river lose them not when they're upside down but after they've come upright: water draining from the helmet washes contacts out. To keep water from draining over your face, wear one of those duck-billed neoprene sun guards or a baseball cap; you can wear either under your helmet without any trouble. You risk losing anything you wear over your helmet.

TWO

Boating Basics

ONCE YOU'RE PROPERLY OUTFITTED, you can move on to some paddling fundamentals. These kayaking basics provide a solid foundation. Smooth, effective technique starts here and is the long-term goal; one efficient stroke is equal to several sloppy ones. Any new techniques you learn will be founded on the following basic elements.

Holding Your Paddle

Curved and offset blades are standard on all performance paddles. Blade curvature imparts more power to a stroke than a flat blade, but it does make proper paddle control a little confusing at first. The concave side of the paddle is called the power face, and the opposite, or convex side, the nonpower face. A paddle is always held so that during a forward stroke, the power face is pointed toward the stern, or rear of the boat.

Because of the offset and curve, you need a strategy to make sure both blades enter the water with their power faces pointed back. Without such a system, one blade may slice through the water, offer no resistance, and possibly cause you to tip. Here's the strategy: one hand, designated the control hand, maintains a firm grip on the paddle shaft and rotates the shaft within the other hand (the noncontrol hand) so that the correct blade angle occurs on both sides. Depending on the blade orientation, paddles are controlled with either the left or the right hand. Most paddles on the market are right-hand controlled. The control hand grips the paddle so that the wrist and forearm are at 90 degrees to the blade, with the power face pointed back. To place the opposite, noncontrol, blade correctly, cock your control wrist out while maintaining the control grip. Keep in mind, for later reference, that there are times when you'll want to cock your control wrist in.

It's not necessarily the case that left-handers should automatically paddle left-control. Some instructors go so far as to maintain that a paddler's dominant hand should be the noncontrol hand.

Beginners somtimes mistakenly rotate the shaft partially within both hands. This causes blade disorientation because the permanent reference grasp that the control hand is meant to provide gets compromised. In addition, rotating the shaft within both hands makes it difficult to do some of the more precise strokes. If you're having this trouble, try a visualization exercise and imagine that there's Super Glue bonding your control hand to the shaft.

An oval shaft (instead of a round shaft), at least in the area around the control hand, facilitates the correct positioning of the control hand and gives you more control over the blade angle with strokes such as the draw and the duffek (Chapter Three). In addition, an oval shaft gives you a better grip and slightly more leverage with your control hand. If you already have a

When viewed from above, a right-control paddle is held as shown. The control forearm is held at 90 degrees to the vertical right blade. This right-control grip remains in place, and the paddle rotates within the left hand as it dips from one side to the other.

RIGHT-HAND CONTROL PADDLE

LEFT BLADE   RIGHT BLADE

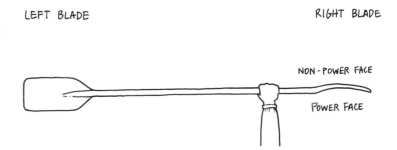

NON-POWER FACE

POWER FACE

WRIST PLACEMENTS

COCKED OUT

COCKED IN

The setting of the control wrist affects blade angle. To correctly place the noncontrol blade in the water, the control hand needs to be cocked out for most strokes. The lower wrist is always in the cocked-out position when draws and duffeks are being done.

round shaft, you can make it oval in the control area by applying a thick line of Shoe Goo or some contoured fiberglass putty. You can even improvise an oval by placing a popsicle stick on the nonpower face side of the shaft. A wrapping of electrical tape will secure the stick and provide a good grip.

HAND PLACEMENT. Proper hand placement on the paddle is important, and there's a general rule of thumb for hand positioning. With the paddle set horizontally on top of your head, your forearms should form close to an 85-degree angle with your upper arms. Where your hands actually find their place on the paddle depends on your own anatomy, but outside this narrow range, power and control are lost if your hands are too close together, and effective paddle reach is reduced if your hands are too far apart. Check your hand positioning by looking in a mirror, by putting your back to the sun and looking at your shadow, or by having a friend check it for you.

Another rule of hand placement is that each hand should be the same distance from the nearer blade. This allows you to execute strokes with the same amount of power on each side. If your hand spread is uneven one side will have more leverage than the other and the boat will tend to turn to the opposite side

To find the correct hand placement, hold the paddle on top of your head and form an angle slightly less than 90 degrees at each elbow. Make sure your hands are equidistant from the tip of the nearest blade.

HOLDING THE PADDLE: THE 90° RULE

when paddling forward—a very frustrating and common phenomenon for novices. To alleviate this, put some electrical tape around the shaft to mark the correct hand position; this way, you can maintain the correct grip without constantly resorting to a visual check. For most people, it's the noncontrol hand that tends to travel toward the middle of the shaft, so you may only need to tape the inside part of the grip, the area next to your thumbs. This is a good tip even for advanced paddlers who often have such a traveling hand.

Strokes

Remember Newton's third law? For every action there is an equal and opposite reaction. The force you impart to the paddle is what makes the boat go where you want it to. With every stroke, energy is transferred from your paddle, through you, and finally to the boat's hull. Knowing how to direct this force is the key to good stroke technique. The basic idea is easy: pull the blade toward you in line with the direction you want to go.

Because the deepest part of the boat is at the center (where you're sitting) and there's less resistance to the water toward the higher ends of the boat, a kayak spins best around its midpoint. This is why you want your boat to be evenly trimmed. Any stroke you do will cause the boat to spin at its midpoint. You can adjust the speed and degree of your spin by varying how far from the boat you do the stroke (A spin refers to the twisting of a boat while it's in place. A turn, on the other hand, is a spin while the boat is moving.). For example, a stroke done far off to the side (a sweep) will turn the boat sharply, but a stroke made close to the side (a forward stroke) will maximize forward propulsion. Putting the blade farther off to the side increases the length of your lever arm, just as increased torque is obtained by using a longer wrench.

Maximize paddle force both by using your muscles to best advantage and by applying the correct blade angle.

VERTICAL AND FLAT BLADES. There are three main categories of strokes: propulsion strokes, turning strokes, and recovery strokes. A proper propulsion or turning stroke requires a vertical blade, perpendicular to the water's surface to effectively transmit force. Recovery maneuvers, on the other hand, call for a flat blade, parallel to the water's surface, because a maximum amount of blade surface needs to come into contact with as much surface water as possible to aid in recovery. Naturally, there are hybridizations of all these strokes, but more about all that in the next chapter.

STATIC AND DYNAMIC STROKES. Propulsion strokes can be either dynamic or static. The term *dynamic* refers to a stroke that moves through the water in relation to the boat. Conversely, a *static* stroke remains in place once inserted, even though you, the water, or both may exert force on it. Most propulsion and turning strokes are dynamic, but a static stroke that has water hitting against it can move the boat around even though the blade itself does not move. Examples of this include ferrying across the river on a stern draw and surfing a wave on a rudder stroke.

POSTURE. You'll usually want to sit upright in your boat when doing propulsion strokes. This position allows you to twist your trunk and abdomen, where most of your power comes from. Sitting up allows you the greatest range of motion and keeps your weight in the middle of the boat where it spins easily. Keep your head up so that you can see and breathe well. Leaning either forward or backward for long periods will interfere with your ability to do strokes effectively. Of course, there are times when leaning either forward or backward is advantageous. Some of these situations are discussed in later sections.

Whenever you're performing maneuvers, you need to brace yourself in the boat by pushing against the foot and knee braces. This gives you a snug fit and efficiently transfers force to the boat.

MAXIMIZING PHYSIOLOGICAL EFFECTIVENESS. When applying power to a stroke, use all your strength and leverage in the muscles that will do some good. Don't indulge in stroke overkill by flexing every muscle in your body. If you use only partial strength, however, you'll get only partial results. Just as you shouldn't start a lawn mower by bending at the waist and pulling with only your biceps, neither should you limit your paddling to your arms. Get full use of all the muscles that contribute to the stroke, primarily the muscles in the arms and torso and, to a lesser extent, the muscles of the thighs and calves.

Use all available leverage; don't cheat yourself. When doing strokes, completely extend your arms to take full advantage of your leverage.

RELAXING. It may come as a surprise to learn that muscle relaxation is also essential to good, efficient technique. Relaxing gives you small opportunities to rest as well as the chance to feel what the water is doing to your boat.

If you're paddling hard for any significant distance, relaxing between strokes will help your circulation and your paddling efficiency. Keep your head upright and breathe regularly. If you're paddling forward, inhale as you stroke on one side and exhale on the other. This rhythm of stroking and breathing will improve your performance.

BALANCING AND LEANING THE BOAT. When you're relaxed, you balance best. If you keep your body and spine rigid, you'll teeter when your boat does—and this may cause a flip. By relaxing your stomach muscles, you can separate your upper body from your boat and lower body. This separation allows the boat to wobble and wiggle while your upper body remains steady. Don't feel as though you have to be rigidly in control every instant.

Leaning the boat intentionally is another important aspect of paddling. Leans can keep you from flipping and are used when executing most river maneuvers. The trick is to lean the boat, not your body. This point can't be overemphasized. The beginner thinks of leaning as bending out over the side of the boat, but this leads to instability and tipping.

The way to lean the boat intentionally is to lift up with one knee and push down on the seat with your opposite buttock. Keep your upper and lower halves separate, just as you do to stay balanced in your boat. When you first try this, you'll feel wobbly and will be able to hold the boat at an angle only momentarily. But with some practice you'll gain strength and balance and will be able to hold the boat on edge for some time. This is well worth practicing, even for advanced paddlers, since it improves balance and boat control immensely.

As you're leaning the boat, you'll have to bend sideways at the waist to maintain your center of gravity; you'll be sitting upright relative to the water, but tilted in relation to the boat. Don't think your upper body needs to remain perpendicular to your deck. Keep your body over the midline of the boat, not over one side or the other. The more the boat's angled, the more you'll have to bend. This can be a hard pose to hold, but it's easier when you have some boat speed—like balancing a bicycle when it's at a standstill as opposed to when it's moving.

BLADE ANGLES. The blade angle and the direction in which the blade is being pulled are the two factors that determine your course. Other variables aside (current, wind, previous motion), the boat will move in the direction of force application. You'll get more force from a blade that presents the most surface area to the direction of force application. If the blade is angled, the blade's effective surface area becomes

BASIC BOAT LEAN

When leaning a boat, keep your body upright. Your center of gravity should stay in the boat's midline, where you're most stable. Loose hips are the key.

As a boat moves through the water, the blade will first push some water down, then push water directly back, and then lift some water up. The more vertical your paddle is when doing propulsion and turning strokes, the more effective your efforts will be.

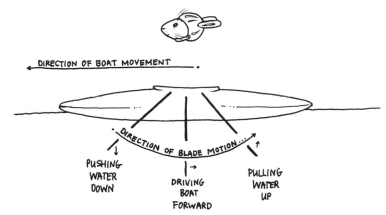

DIRECTION OF BOAT MOVEMENT

DIRECTION OF BLADE MOTION

PUSHING WATER DOWN

DRIVING BOAT FORWARD

PULLING WATER UP

reduced and you'll lose power. As you'll see in later chapters, however, there are times when changing your blade angle is necessary and advantageous.

To get the most from a propulsion or a turning stroke, you need to orient the blade perpendicularly to the pull and to the water's surface. This way all your power will go into moving the boat. When the blade is angled power face down and you pull on it, some of your energy will go into depressing water as well as moving you forward. And if the blade's power face is angled up on a stroke, you'll be lifting water. Either way is inefficient. Since your goal is to move the boat along the surface, not to compress or raise the river, keep your propulsion strokes vertical.

USING THE WHOLE BLADE. With any stroke, you need to immerse the blade in the water. If the blade isn't completely submerged, potential power is lost; if you use only half the paddle, you'll get only half the results. But neither should you drown your blade, as this reduces your reach and stroke efficiency. No matter which stroke you use, insert the blade to the throat (where the blade meets the shaft) but no farther.

THREE

Propulsion and Turning Strokes

PROPULSION AND TURNING STROKES ARE YOUR TICKET to maneuvering through rapids. The more effectively you can execute them, the easier and more enjoyable river-running will be. The better your stroke technique, the more options you'll have on the river. In this chapter, all strokes are described in their complete and pure form; on a river, circumstances usually cause you to adjust and blend them to achieve your desired outcome. In fact, on the river, pure strokes are relatively rare. You must, however, master them before they can be adapted to suit the situation at hand. Fluency with pure strokes is essential for the development of good technique. Make sure that these paddling basics are automatic and technically solid before spending a lot of time on more advanced maneuvers.

Some strokes are relatively easy to learn, but others, like the duffek, are mastered only with time and practice. Even advanced paddlers often have flaws in their basic stroke technique that keep them from improving beyond a certain level. Therefore it's good to review the stroke basics occasionally to make sure you're still on track. Keep in mind that although one minor technical flaw may not seem important, the cumulative effect of several flaws can be significant.

The Forward Stroke

The forward stroke is the most commonly used stroke and is, in many ways, the foundation of paddling technique; it moves the boat more efficiently than any other stroke. It's easy to learn the rudiments of the forward stroke, but it's also easy to develop bad habits. If you spend time perfecting the forward stroke early on, you'll be amply rewarded. For advanced paddlers stuck at a plateau, reviewing these basics may give your performance a boost.

The forward stroke can be divided into four parts: the setup, the catch, the power phase, and the exit. This division is only a guideline for analysis; if you take it too seriously, your forward stroke will be segmented and jerky.

THE SETUP. The setup is the foundation of a good forward stroke. Make your wrists form a basically horizontal plane with the shoulders. The elbow of your upper arm will be in this plane, but the other elbow (the one that's cocked and close to the shoulder) will sit below. Extend your pulling arm far forward by rotating your shoulders, torso, and abdomen. If you flex this same knee up, you'll help rotate your hip forward. This, in turn, will help twist your torso and shoulders into the correct setup position. The hand of the extended arm needs to be over the boat's midline. When you extend your paddle by twisting your torso, you're arranging your body to allow the powerful muscles of your back and abdomen to be unleashed later

The forward stroke setup. Notice the upright body position and the slight twist of the torso. The right arm is straight, allowing the blade to be placed far forward.

A left catch. This shot was taken an instant after the true catch—some power has been applied; thus, the bent left arm. The right arm is being straightened as it punches forward at forehead level.

during the power phase; you're storing energy. Tempting as it may be, don't bend at the waist to get a good forward reach, since this will channel some of your energy into making the bow bob down into the water.

THE CATCH. A good catch is critical for maximum power and efficiency because it places the blade in the vertical position necessary for the effective application of power. A solid catch gives the blade a firm grip on the water so that the boat moves forward in relation to the stationary blade: in effect, it allows you to move the boat toward the paddle rather than vice versa.

From the setup position, a combination of a downward movement with the pulling arm and a forward thrust with the pushing (upper) arm will immerse the blade. This upper-arm punch is accomplished by thrusting straight out with your top hand, from a level even with your shoulder to a level about even with your forehead. Avoid punching higher than your head or lower than your nose. If you're practicing the forward stroke on flat water, aim your punch at the horizon. Keep the blade close to the boat, since the farther from the boat you place the stroke, the more it will cause the boat to veer off course. Strive for a splashless catch: if you stab the blade cleanly into the water, you don't waste energy and the blade has the correct vertical orientation. A very slight sideways motion with the blade as you immerse it facilitates a smooth insertion.

THE POWER PHASE. Now you apply power to the paddle. If you're performing the forward stroke correctly, the majority of your power comes from the untwisting of your torso. The pull from the lower arm also contributes to the force of the stroke; the push from the upper arm contributes least because it has already been mostly extended to achieve the catch.

As you pull on the paddle with your lower arm, keep the paddle shaft perpendicular to your wrist and keep your lower forearm parallel to the water surface. The paddle should remain fairly vertical throughout the stroke. In addition, remember to keep the blade square to your direction of travel—forward. Maintain the blade's throat at surface level. Also, continue to keep the blade close to the boat throughout the stroke so that the boat turns minimally. As you apply power to the paddle, visualize having set the blade in concrete (during your catch) so that the boat, not the blade, moves through the water. Inserting the blade as far forward as possible (without bending at the waist) increases the distance traveled with each stroke.

THE EXIT. Taking the blade out of the water is easy enough; the trick is in the timing. If you take it out too early, you cheat yourself of some power, and if you take it out late, the blade drags, slowing the boat. In addition, if you drag the blade you pull water up in order to get the paddle out. This is a nonproductive use of energy, and it causes your stern to sink slightly, slowing you even more.

Near the end of the power phase. The right arm is now completely extended and has dropped from forehead to shoulder level.

A right exit. The blade is taken out of the water just past the hip. Even here, the blade inefficiently lifts up a little water. The left arm is extended in preparation for another stroke. Note the twisting of the torso to prepare for the placement of the next stroke.

To exit at the correct time, start pulling the blade out of the water when your lower hand becomes even with your hip. Lifting up some water is unavoidable but try to minimize it. To avoid slowing the boat with your blade exit, try taking the blade out by pulling it out slightly to the side, away from the boat. By lifting your lower hand up, to a position right in front of the same shoulder, you assume the now familiar setup position for the next stroke on the other side. It's time for another forward stroke!

HOW TO GO STRAIGHT. If you're having problems keeping the boat going straight while paddling forward, keep in mind that all paddlers have the same problem—even if they're pros. Experts are just exceptionally quick at anticipating and correcting the boat's veering before it becomes malignant. They keep the boat flat from side to side, perform subtle leans to correct for the boat's veering, and incorporate almost invisible correctional draws and sweeps (discussed later) into their forward stroke. These techniques are useful for beginners as well as advanced paddlers; novices have problems going straight in flat water and more advanced boaters often have the same problems in white water.

Since whitewater boats are so responsive, even an Olympic-perfect forward stroke will turn the boat from side to side to a small extent. Going straight is so frustrating because it seems it should be so easy. It's especially difficult when you're moving against the current. Novice paddlers tend to get discouraged, thinking, "Jeez, if I can't do this, I'm going to be history on the river!" But keep at it. After a few hours of flatwater paddling, you'll find your technique mysteriously improving.

UNEVEN LEVERAGE. Unintentional veering can occur when one of your arms is stronger then the other (your throwing arm, for example). You may tend, unconsciously, to execute a more powerful stroke on your stronger side. It's also common to see a paddler, even a very good one, hold the noncontrol hand closer to the shaft's midpoint (the traveling hand syndrome mentioned in Chapter Two). This causes more leverage to be imparted to a stroke done on the non-control side. Increased leverage on one side causes the boat to turn to the opposite direction. If this is a recurring problem, put some tape around the shaft at your correct grip locations (see Chapter Two).

LEANING WHILE GLIDING. Leaning your moving boat will cause it to turn. Knowledge of this principle is valuable when you're starting out; it can help you keep the boat going straight. It also comes into play in subtle ways with numerous advanced techniques. To get a feeling for this, paddle in a straight line to get up some speed, then stop paddling and lean the boat as you continue gliding. If you play around with this, you may notice something interesting; sometimes the boat veers to the left when you lean right, and other times it goes left when you lean left. A lean to the same side that the boat turns is called an on-side lean; a lean to the opposite side is termed an off-side lean.

Notice that the quality of each turn is different. A turn with an on-side, or inside, lean tends to be smooth and wide and maintains its glide for a while, whereas a turn with an off-side, or outside, lean is sharper and relatively abrupt, and the boat's speed drops off fairly quickly.

The way the boat veers depends on the boat's momentum. This is usually, but not always, determined by which side your last stroke was made on; if your last stroke was on the left, the boat almost always turns to the right after you stop paddling, and vice versa. Sometimes, however, previous momentum in one direction is too strong and a stroke on the opposite side isn't enough to cancel or overcome it; if you're just learning to paddle forward, previous momentum, whatever the etiology, is a major reason why the boat veers from side to side, seemingly with a mind of its own.

CORRECTING IN TIME. The hardest thing to learn is to recognize and correct the boat's veering before you're too far off course. At this point it becomes nearly impossible to correct without coming to a near stop. Atune yourself to subtle shifts in the boat's momentum. With practice, you'll be able to feel them before the boat actually starts turning. If you catch the veer before it goes wild, lean to the same side; this helps diminish the veer. If you need to (and chances are you will), you can also do a small correctional stroke: a small sweep, a small bow draw (later in this chapter), or another forward stroke on the same side. If your correction stroke is too strong, you will have to correct for your correction on the other side, thus wasting additional energy. Try to do your corrections as early as possible and make them as small as you can. Taking two or more strokes in a row on the same side is a perfectly fair way of correcting a veer.

PADDLING SMOOTHLY. Now for fine-tuning. As you stroke on each side of the boat, your weight shifts from side to side. This lateral rocking is unavoidable to some extent but should be minimized as it wastes energy. Why rock the boat from side to side when you can channel that same force into moving forward? As they say, "Don't rock the boat." In addition, don't lean forward when you plant the blade, and don't lean back as you take it out. Bobbing forward does give you a bit more reach with the paddle, but it inhibits a good torso twist and causes the boat to rock from front to back. More wasted energy.

To keep the boat moving smoothly, make a quick transition from the exit to the catch—you want to do the next stroke just before the boat starts slowing from the previous stroke. Don't rush to insert the next stroke; just make sure that you're not pausing. If your

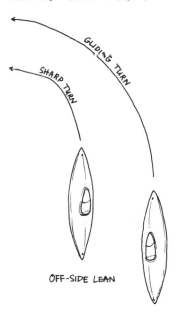

Boats turn differently depending on which way they are leaned. A off-side lean produces a somewhat sharper turn than an on-side lean.

timing is right, the boat will travel smoothly, without a jerky stop-and-go motion. To practice this, try paddling in slow motion on flat water. Concentrate first on perfecting each phase of the forward stroke. Then, without speeding up, let the parts flow together in one continuous, graceful motion.

CRAMPED FOREARMS. A common paddler's complaint is cramped forearms, caused by gripping the shaft too tightly. This is sometimes a sign of nervousness, but it also occurs when a paddler is using a round shaft. A round shaft makes it difficult to judge the blade's exact position; you'll tend to ensure proper hand placement by gripping the paddle harder than necessary. Cramping caused by a too-tight grip can be helped by opening the last three fingers of the hand that's in the upper position as it extends forward. This still allows the thumb and index finger to hold the shaft, since only the lower hand is necessary to maintain a grip on the shaft. You can use this technique with each stroke to restore circulation to your forearms. If a round shaft is causing tightness, switch to an oval shaft, which is easier to grip.

The Reverse Stroke

Picture a forward stroke, only in reverse. The main difference is that you can't insert the blade as far from your body as you can when doing a forward stroke. The blade is inserted a foot or so behind your hip and is taken out about 2 feet in front of your body. To make insertion easier, slide the blade in a little from the side before applying power. Don't put the paddle in too far behind you or you'll end up pushing a lot of water down.

It's pretty easy to get the basic idea of the reverse stroke, but if you had a hard time keeping the boat going straight while paddling forward you'll be particularly frustrated now. Because it's hard to see where you're going, the boat will get farther off track before you realize it. It's also hard to gauge how much correction is needed. To make it easy on yourself, you'll have a tendency (everyone does) to insert wimpy little reverse sweep strokes out to the side—this drives you backward, but not very efficiently. To do proper reverse strokes, keep the paddle vertical and close to the boat.

When you need to correct, put in a reverse sweep at the beginning of a stroke.

Avoid turning your head from side to side as you paddle backward: look back over only one shoulder. Otherwise you'll get disoriented from the swiveling, and by the time you adjust to the new perspective, it'll be time to switch back.

The sweep is the most basic of the turning strokes. It's also the easiest to do. The sweep stroke turns the boat while allowing it to maintain momentum, so you'll find it useful in situations where it's important to keep up your forward speed as you change your course. As always, a good fit in the boat is important. If the fit isn't good, your sweep will just twist you, rather than turn the boat.

There are two parts to the sweep stroke. These are usually combined into one fluid motion but can be done independently if the situation demands. For a right-hand sweep, the first part of the stroke begins at the front of the boat (twelve o'clock) and ends at the three o'clock position: it turns the boat by pushing the front of the boat away from the paddle blade. The second part continues the motion from the three o'clock position and ends at the stern. This second component continues turning the boat, but here you effect the turn by pulling the stern toward the blade. This is called a stern draw. This may seem like an artificial distinction, but the two parts of the sweep *do* have different applications, depending on context.

SOME SWEEP PRELIMINARIES. With the forward stroke you attempt to keep the boat from veering, but with the sweep, you try to maximize the veer. This difference results primarily from a difference in the angle of the paddle shaft relative to the water's surface: with the forward stroke, the shaft is vertical, whereas the sweep requires the paddle shaft to be almost horizontal. This serves to maximize the distance of the blade from the side of the boat at the apex of the sweep's arc. The farther the paddle blade is from the boat, the more leverage there is to turn the boat. Again, to get the most from the sweep, use the muscles of your arms and torso, not just your arms.

The Sweep Stroke

EXECUTING THE SWEEP. In a correct sweep, you plant the blade as close to the bow as possible without leaning your body forward. To do it, you must twist your torso. The sweep, like the forward stroke, gets its power when the chest and abdominal muscles are unleashed. Extend your sweep, or lower, arm fully to get this forward placement, with the hand on the sweeping side about 6 inches lower than the other hand. During the sweep, the lower arm remains fully extended and the plane of the shoulder follows the arc of the blade. The sweeping blade thus travels nearly 180 degrees from bow to stern. Start by placing the upper hand in front of its corresponding pectoralis muscle, with the arm in a cocked position. As the blade makes its arc, extend your upper, or pushing, arm diagonally across your chest. The key is synchronization. At the end of the stroke, when the blade is against the stern, both arms should be nearly straight with the paddle parallel to the boat's side. Throughout the entire sweep, the line of your shoulders should remain fairly parallel with the paddle shaft. If you keep your shoulders even with the shaft throughout the sweep, you'll get a good untwisting of your torso muscles. You don't need to be neurotically concerned about attaining God's Perfect Torso Twist; if there's good lower-arm extension and blade placement—without bending forward at the waist—the correct amount of torso twist will follow.

A common mistake is often made at the end of the sweep, when the blade is at the stern. You may be tempted to end the stroke leaning back on the deck to get a larger arc and more leverage. Don't. Your body will be left in an awkward, unstable position and you won't be ready to react to whatever comes next—bad news in white water. For the most part, stay upright. Leaning forward while doing a sweep, however, is sometimes advantageous on the river; you get greater reach from bow and your lowered position gives you added stability.

KEEPING THE BLADE UNDERWATER AND VERTICAL. Be aware of what the blade is doing as it sweeps through the water. Keep it completely—but barely—under the water's surface throughout the arc.

The start of the sweep. The paddle is horizontal in comparison with the forward stroke. The blade is inserted close to the bow by twisting and straightening the arm completely. Note how near the arms are to the top of the deck. The boater is sitting upright and the left arm is initially quite close to the body.

The midpoint. The right arm is still straight to allow the blade to achieve maximum distance from the boat's side. The left arm pushes forward and diagonally across the chest to add power to the sweep.

The exit. Allow the blade to come close to the stern before taking it out. By this time, both arms are nearly straight and the body is still upright. Notice that the torso is now twisted in the opposite direction that it was at sweep's beginning.

Otherwise, a portion of the blade will push air instead of water, and once again, you'll lose power. Conversely, if the blade is too far below the surface, the paddle shaft will be more vertical than the optimal sweep position requires, and an inefficient forward stroke rather than a good sweep will result.

Maintain a vertical blade the whole distance of the arc. Because of the way our bodies are built, there's a tendency to turn the blade power face up toward the end of the sweep. That lifts water and wastes energy.

USING YOUR WHOLE BODY. Make sure to put your abdominal, shoulder, and back muscles into the sweep—they're all strong muscles. The sweep will be compromised if performed with the arms alone. While you sweep, lift up your corresponding knee to gain some additional power. Visualize planting your blade in concrete, as you did with the forward stroke, and use the whole of your body to twist your boat around the fixed blade.

WATCHING THE SWEEP. Watching the entire sweep helps you learn it faster, but after the motions become automatic, stop looking. The sweep needs to be a familiar kinesthetic motion. Your eyes should be free to look ahead to where the action is. When you stop watching, however, make sure your torso twist doesn't diminish.

THE OUTSIDE LEAN. Remember that your boat will turn more sharply when leaned to the outside. So if you lean the boat minimally to the side of your sweep, you'll produce a slightly faster and snappier turn. If you lean too much, however, the boat may stall.

The Reverse Sweep

Picture a forward sweep, only in . . . The reverse sweep is very much like the forward sweep, but it's still worth practicing. You should remember those details that are old hat by now: twist your torso, keep your sweep arm straight, pull (don't push) your other arm diagonally across your chest, keep the blade vertical and just under the surface, arc the blade out as far as possible, and stay upright. To do the reverse sweep, insert the blade as close to the stern as possible and arc it 180 degrees, taking it out at the bow. Simple.

The Rudder

The rudder position is basically the same position you're in before you take the forward sweep out of the water. Don't let the blade touch the boat. Your hands are low (you're holding a horizontal paddle), your "lower" arm is nearly straight, and your upper arm is fairly bent. Both hands are over the same side of the boat. The rudder is sort of an intentional dragging of a vertical blade through the water.

To rudder, hold the paddle close to the stern—6 inches is about right. Keep the whole blade in the water and vertical. From this position, you can turn the boat one way by doing a stern draw, or the other way by pushing the blade away from your stern—a reverse sweep. The utility of the rudder is especially apparent when wave surfing, where it allows you to cut powerfully across a wave face.

The Draw

No other stroke has as many variations and permutations as the draw. And few strokes are as versatile. The plain old generic side draw is done at the three o'clock position and is used to pull the boat sideways. But if a draw is done near the bow or stern, it acts as a turning stroke. The draw is the precursor of the duffek stroke and is combined with many feathering moves—advanced techniques for doing multiple strokes without taking the blade out of the water.

DOING THE SIDE DRAW. To perform an effective side draw, insert the blade as far from the side of the boat as possible. Place it even with your hip and position the paddle as vertical as you can by pushing your top arm across—or slightly above—your forehead. The top hand should be more or less over the lower hand. Yes, this is initially quite awkward, since the boat and the body need to stay upright; it feels a bit like you're on a medieval rack. You'll have to bend your lower arm slightly to get the paddle fairly vertical. Doing a torso twist, which allows you to face the paddle will also help. Lift up with your corresponding knee to keep the boat level; otherwise, the boat will have a tendency to lean into the direction of your draw, which can destabilize you. The drawing blade needs to

The side draw. Extend the paddle, placing the blade out as far as possible from the side. When the blade is pulled, the boat will travel sideways toward the blade. Note the position of the forearm and the forehead.

be in the water about 2 feet from the boater's side, but absolutely no less than 1½ feet.

Complete the draw by pulling it straight in toward your hip. Stop pulling on it as it gets 6 or so inches from the boat, and rotate the blade 90 degrees by cocking your wrist in, as though you're doing wrist curls with weights. From this position, slide the paddle back out through the water to your original starting place, straighten your wrist (bringing the blade parallel to the boat) and draw the paddle in again. This exercise helps teach you the draw and prepares the way for future feathering techniques. Try not to let the draw hit the side of the boat. If you let the blade go under the boat with any speed, the boat's side will act like a fulcrum and you may tip over. Since your top arm is already out to the side, you're in a somewhat precarious position. Beware, but don't be so cautious that you end up not extending your upper arm.

DRAWING WHILE FEATHERING. Feathering is the technique of sliding your blade through the water so that you can move it without taking it out of the water. The feathering draw is another version of the side draw but requires more finesse. With this stroke, you can move the boat sideways by slicing the paddle fore and aft. By adjusting the angle that your blade face makes with the boat as you slide the paddle back and forth parallel to the keel, you can exert a force perpendicular to the keel. You're using the paddle blade in much the same way as a sailboat uses its sail to harness the force of a crosswind to move forward.

USING BLADE ANGLES. To do the feathering draw, assume the proper draw position, but this time, place the blade only about 1 to 1½ feet from your hip. Open the blade by turning the power face toward the bow slightly. You open the blade by cocking your wrist out without releasing your control grip (your control wrist opens the blade whether it's in the upper or lower position). Now slide the blade forward to about 2 feet in front of you. Change the blade angle by closing it—cocking your control wrist in—so that the power face is pointing slightly toward the stern. Keep the same blade angle relative to the boat's midline. (When the blade is near the bow, the power face should be oriented toward the bow, and when near the stern, facing the stern.) Slide the blade behind you about 2 feet, maintaining the blade at the same distance from the boat throughout. Move the blade back and forth, changing the blade angle every time it gets to one end of the 4-foot track. It's a tough motion to visualize, but with practice you'll be able to pull the boat sideways with little effort, using smooth transitions at each end. Experiment with the blade angle to find the one that works best.

Avoid leaning the boat into the stroke or you'll spend a lot of energy plowing up water with your boat's vertical sides. Try lifting your knee on the same side you're drawing on, as you did for the basic draw. The more level you keep your boat, the easier it will slide across the surface.

If you have problems keeping the boat going sideways and one end of the boat begins to move ahead of the other, move the draw stroke toward the lagging end until the boat angle is corrected.

BLADE ANGLES

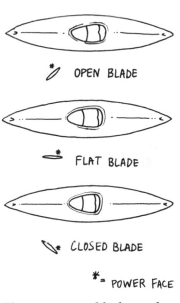

OPEN BLADE

FLAT BLADE

CLOSED BLADE

* = POWER FACE

Changing your blade angle changes the degree of your turn. The more open your blade is (power face forward), the faster you will turn, but the sooner you'll stop. This is one-sided braking action. Use an open or flat blade angle for the bow draw. A flat or closed angle is better for feathering the blade through the water.

The Duffek

In the early fifties, Czechoslovakian slalom racer Milo Duffek (pronounced *dew-feck*) first applied to kayaking the canoe stroke known as the bow draw. The duffek (as it came to be called) didn't gain wide popularity in the slalom world until the early seventies, when its potential was realized, and it became a mandatory skill and the turning stroke of choice for every slalom racer. The stroke was initially a static one—a vertical high brace with an open blade angle. The paddle was used as a pivot point to turn on. But the stroke has evolved and is now often combined with a draw so that the duffek has numerous variations, some static (remains in place), but many dynamic (moves through the water).

THE DUFFEK'S VERSATILITY. The duffek is so useful because, from its position in front of the paddler and out to the boat's side, it can easily be converted into a number of other strokes, including the draw, the forward stroke, and the sweep. The duffek is most often used with eddy turns but is also an excellent steering maneuver capable of smoothly changing the direction of a boat in midstream.

Although the duffek is energy-efficient and versatile, many people hesitate to give it a wholehearted try because of its initial awkwardness. True, it takes longer to see the rewards than with, say, a sweep stroke. But with practice the duffek is extremely effective and almost effortless. The stroke is initially unwieldy for the same reasons that the draw is: both hands are over the same side of the boat, which stretches the forearms uncomfortably and makes the boat feel tippy. Also, the blade is set vertically in the water, giving you nothing to lean on for support.

THE STATIC DUFFEK. This is the no-frills, quintessential duffek that most paddlers initially learn. It's a static stroke, meaning that once you insert the paddle, it remains in place relative to the boat. In this version, the duffek is inserted in the water while you have some speed, and the boat spins around the paddle in the same way you would spin around a signpost. The paddle thus acts as a pivot point.

To do the static duffek, assume the draw position,

but instead of putting the blade directly to your side, put it about 1 foot from your bow. Open the blade to approximately a 45-degree angle. Make sure that your lower arm is almost completely extended and that your top forearm is horizontal and even with your forehead. Get your top hand directly over the side of the boat toward which you are turning. The second photograph in the dynamic duffek sequence shows what the static duffek position should look like.

THE PRETURN. When you're comfortable with the positioning, try doing it with a little bit of speed and a slight inside lean. Prepare for the duffek by doing a small sweep to initiate a slight turn on the same side. This preturn is critical to a good duffek turn. The boat's momentum must already be in the direction that you want to turn. Otherwise an aquatic version of the splits results: the boat continues in one direction, while the duffek feebly attempts to pull it in the other.

Notice that when you place the stroke after you pick up some speed, you do a very smooth, wide, arcing turn. The duffek is functioning just like a rudder—but at the bow—while both paddle and boat move through the water. By adjusting the angle of your blade, you can regulate the sharpness of your turn. The more you open the blade, the faster you'll turn but the quicker you'll stop. If you feel horribly unstable, drop your upper arm a little to get the paddle slightly horizontal. This gives your duffek some brace character and gives you some support from the water surface (see Chapter Four).

THE DYNAMIC DUFFEK. The dynamic duffek, also known as a bow draw, pulls primarily the bow toward the blade (the basic draw, remember, pulls the whole boat toward the paddle). Start with a motionless boat on still water and put the blade out to the side of the boat, directly out from the hip. Stretch both arms over the side to place the paddle vertically. This is the same position as the draw stroke. Now slide the blade forward, with a slightly open blade angle. As you move the blade forward, simultaneously pull the paddle toward the boat. The result is a diagonal movement of the blade toward the bow and a corresponding turn

The bow draw, or dynamic duffek. The body and arm positioning is similar to that of the side draw, except that now the power face is aimed toward the bow. To achieve this position, cock the corresponding wrist out without changing your control grip.

The sweep arm pushes the blade toward the bow; and the boat turns. This is also the position of the static duffek. See how the upper arm position remains unchanged from the previous photo but the lower arm travels from side to front. The body also bends from upright to slightly forward.

Before you take it out of the water, bring the blade close to the bow. This will get the most out of your bow draw.

of the bow toward the blade. Stop moving the blade when it's as far forward as you can comfortably get it (about where the forward stroke is initiated) and about 6 inches from the boat's side.

ADJUSTING YOUR TURN. The faster you execute the bow draw, the quicker the boat will turn. You can also open the blade angle more so that some water is pushed forward. This angle makes a sharper turn, but the open blade also slows or even stalls the boat. You can adjust the stroke to fit the circumstances; but strive for the happy medium that gives a crisp, smooth turn. In white water, it's best to keep the blade parallel to the boat in order to achieve graceful turns.

THE OUTSIDE LEAN. Most of the time you want to lean your boat into the turn, like a bicycle. But if you have a low-volume boat with sharp edges and a hard chine, try leaning away from the turn while you do your static duffek or bow draw. Remember that leaning to the outside will give you a sharper turn. By combining your duffek with an off-side lean, you'll make a turn that is especially crisp.

DUFFEK DEFECTS. There are several mistakes that occur when paddlers attempt the duffek. By far the most common problem is insufficient extension of the upper arm over the opposite side of the boat. If you don't reach over far enough, your paddle shaft won't be vertical. Your top forearm should be horizontal and close to your forehead. Yes, the position feels weird, but if it gets too far in front of you, control is sacrificed.

Since the correct blade angle is not obvious at first, beginners sometimes accidentally put the non-power side of the blade facing the bow. The stroke functions like a reverse stroke inserted at the bow, but with no place to go. Imagine applying the brakes to only one wheel of a car. Sure, you'd turn, but only by completely stopping on one side.

The opposite problem occurs when a paddler inserts the blade at an angle perpendicular to the boat. When the power face is angled completely forward and the boater is moving fast, too much water hits the blade at once, sometimes wrenching the paddle behind the body and leaving the paddler leaning on the back deck. Awkward indeed! If you find yourself lean-ing back after a duffek, this is usually the reason.

Make sure that the whole blade is in the water but not drowned. As with any stroke, it makes no sense to use only half the blade. If it's already correctly in the water, pushing it down farther is overkill.

Combination Strokes

After fluency with pure strokes is mastered, you can move into the more advanced realm of combination strokes. Most paddlers don't practice these strokes, but instead develop them in a somewhat haphazard manner. It's worth your while to practice stroke com-binations on flat water; familiarity with them there will help you on white water. This section touches on a few of the possibilities. Its main function is to help you become aware of some of the ways in which strokes can be blended and mixed.

Combination strokes are valuable because they maximize your efficiency; you can execute two or more stroke functions with one insertion of the paddle blade. Top slalom racers consistently use fewer strokes than less skilled racers to complete a slalom course—and in the fastest time. Strength, correct boat place-ment, and effective water usage help them win, of course. But so does the ability to blend and use strokes effectively.

Combination strokes come in two main forms: hybrid strokes and sequential combinations. A hybrid stroke is an amalgamation of two pure strokes. The clearest, most basic example combines forward and sweep strokes to simultaneously turn and drive the boat ahead.

Sequential combinations are two or more strokes that are done in sequence. They can be accomplished by transforming one stroke into another or by tying full strokes together via feathering—moving the pad-dle around without taking it out of the water.

HYBRID STROKES. These strokes are the easi-est of the combination strokes to master as they don't require feathering or transitions halfway through. Nat-urally, there are several more possibilities than the two mentioned here. Feel free to experiment and design your own combinations.

FORWARD STROKE–SWEEP. Novices tend to perform this hybrid unconsciously in lieu of doing either a distinct forward stroke or a sweep stroke; their forward strokes turn them as much as their sweeps drive them forward. If this is intentional, fine, but not if it's a muddling of two distinct strokes.

To carry out this hybrid stroke correctly, insert the blade at the bow and sweep the paddle out to the side. Don't go for maximum arc distance or you'll get a full-fledged sweep stroke. You can either take the blade out at your hip or continue sweeping it the full 180 degrees.

FORWARD STROKE–DRAW. This is a useful and common hybrid stroke. It's simply a forward stroke that is initiated a foot or two from the bow. It moves the boat simultaneously sideways and forward—diagonally. The blade angle should be closed and at a 45-degree angle to your boat as you pull the paddle toward you. If you do a small duffek before doing this stroke, you'll turn the boat very efficiently, albeit subtly. Take your blade out at your hip, the normal forward stroke exit point.

SEQUENTIAL STROKES AND FEATHERING. These are trickier. The transition from one stroke to another while keeping the blade underwater and still exerting force on the paddle requires some practice. In addition, sequential strokes are often blended via feathering, which takes a bit of practice.

If you're effectively doing the draw strokes described earlier, you already know, basically, how to feather your blade through the water. Feathering allows you to make fine steering adjustments by changing the angle of the blade relative to the side of the boat while turning or moving. In addition, feathering increases your stability and helps keep you on track. Since your blade helps support you like an outrigger, you'll be more stable. Also, whenever your blade is in the water, it's harder for the water to push your boat around on the water's surface.

FORWARD STROKE–FORWARD STROKE. Here's a relatively simple one. You just take a normal forward stroke, but instead of taking the blade out at your hip, you bring it parallel to the boat. Then slide the blade back up to the forward stroke catch position. This combination is used when one forward stroke isn't quite enough to take you in the direction you want or if there's no need to put in a stroke on the other side. The biggest advantage of feathering between two forward strokes is that you can open the blade while sliding it back up to the bow. This turns your second forward stroke into a bit of a bow draw, allowing you to adjust your boat direction slightly.

Both forward strokes can be full strokes, or either can be partial, depending on the situation.

FORWARD STROKE–STERN DRAW. With a forward stroke, you normally take the blade out at your hip. With the forward stroke–stern draw you push the blade out from the boat by lowering your top arm when the blade is even with your hip. Continue by doing a stern draw. (The stern draw is described in the sweep section).

This combination stroke drives the boat forward initially but then suddenly turns it halfway through. Do the transition between the forward stroke and the stern draw quickly and smoothly, applying force to the paddle throughout. Avoid doing one stage, pausing, and then doing the next. That pause will cause the boat to slow down and you'll have to exert more strength to turn the boat.

DUFFEK–FORWARD STROKE. This is another good combination stroke to have in your array of options, as it's useful for changing your boat direction in midcurrent as well as for eddy turns. With experience, this will become one of your bread-and-butter strokes on the river. The duffek turns the boat and the forward stroke comes into action just as the momentum of the boat is starting to dwindle.

To execute this stroke, do any version of the duffek. When the blade gets near the bow, rotate the blade nearly 90 degrees so that the power face is pointed toward your stern—the forward stroke position. Since your body position for the finish of a duffek is almost exactly the same as for a forward stroke catch, it's an easy transition to make. Your forward stroke can be either a full stroke or a partial one, depending on circumstance and destination.

DUFFEK-SWEEP. The duffek–sweep combination is especially useful for doing S turns across an eddy (Chapter Six). It is akin to the duffek–forward stroke, but the upper arm is quickly lowered when the duffek ends, to set the stage for a forward sweep instead of a forward stroke. This stroke makes the boat follow an S-shaped path; the duffek pulls the boat toward the blade and a sweep or stern draw then pushes the bow the other way. To achieve a fluid motion, make a smooth transition between strokes. Be aware that the more you turn the boat with the duffek, the harder it will be to change the boat's momentum in the opposite direction with your sweep. A partial duffek therefore is the best choice.

FOUR

Recovery Strokes and Maneuvers

WITH GOOD RECOVERY TECHNIQUE, you can frolic and play on the river without dreading a long, cold, exhausting swim. The more you play the river, the better a paddler you'll become. Your greater paddling proficiency will, in turn, keep you from flipping as frequently. This will be a great relief to both you and your rescue-weary friends.

There are two kinds of braces, low and high, to help you avoid capsizing. There are also a variety of ways to do a roll, which serves to right you after you've tipped over. Essential to all recovery techniques is a good hip snap.

The Hip Snap

Bracing and rolling require less physical effort if you have good hip action. During a brace, the hip snap helps to keep the boat flat on the water. When rolling, snap your hips first to bring the boat up. Once the boat is up, it's easy for you to come out of the water.

The hip snap is sort of a glorified boat lean. Basically, you lift up with one knee and push down with the opposite buttock. While upright, you can practice this by rocking the boat from side to side using the leans described in Chapter Two. Keep your upper body isolated from the motion of the boat and try to stay as

The hip snap. Although it goes against instinct, keep your head down while hip snapping. This makes it easier to right the boat, since your head and shoulders are lighter in water than in air.

HIP SNAP

RIGHT: HEAD KEPT DOWN

upright as possible, even when the boat is on edge. If you've ever performed a hula or a belly dance, you'll be good at this.

RIGHTING THE BOAT. The best way to practice a full-fledged hip snap is in a pool or with a friend in shallow water. Grab the pool side or the paddle shaft that your friend is holding at water level parallel to the boat. Flip over while holding on to the pool side or paddle. Keep your head and trunk underwater and, while looking at the bottom of the pool or your friend's feet, flick your hips to right the boat. Once the boat is up, you can bring up your torso and, finally, your head. To right the boat and keep your head under, you'll have to bend sideways at the waist. Make sure that your head stays under until last; it'll make coming up infinitely easier. For comparison, intentionally bring your head up first—notice how much you have to muscle your way up! This is because your head and shoulders weigh more in air than they do in water. If you're persistently bringing your head up first (the most common error in roll technique), have a friend gently put a hand on your head to remind you to keep it down.

HIP SNAP

WRONG : HEAD UP TOO SOON

The incorrect hip snap. Notice how lifting the head too soon levers the boat upside down, making the hip snap a test of strength rather than technique.

The Low Brace

While you perform the low brace, your arms and elbows are held above the paddle shaft, which should be horizontal at belly-button level. A low brace puts the nonpower side of the blade in contact with the surface of the water. The low brace is extremely effective, up to a point. It provides excellent initial stability, but if the boat tips over too far, it loses its righting capability.

PRACTICING THE LOW BRACE. Hold the paddle just above your sprayskirt, with your elbows slightly behind you and next to your sides. Now, lean the boat by lifting abruptly up with one knee while leaning your body out over the side of the boat—in other words, tip the boat. To recover from an imminent flip, quickly slap the water with the nonpower face of the blade and pull it back to the starting position by sliding the blade toward the boat. If you keep the blade moving on the surface, it won't sink. The farther you can comfortably extend the blade to the side, the greater your leverage (as with a forward sweep). As you slap the water, lift up with the knee that's on the side you're flipping toward and simultaneously snap your hips. This compensatory hip snap helps bring the

The low brace is a very stable recovery stroke. The power face is up and the elbows are above the paddle shaft. Keep the paddle close to your body to get the most leverage.

LOW BRACE

boat upright. Done together, these two motions give you a bombproof low brace.

Notice the natural tendency to thrust your head and upper body upright when you start to flip. This motion defuses the hip snap and tips the boat over even farther.

Some additional tips: the faster you slap the blade against the water, the less time there will be for the blade to sink. Make sure your shoulder is directly over the bracing hand, which affords you the optimal mechanical advantage for pushing your paddle onto the surface. It's analogous to doing push-ups; you do them best when your shoulders are over your hands. Finally, keep the paddle close to your body and your bracing elbow directly over the paddle shaft. Your paddle should be rubbing against your life jacket; the farther the paddle is in front of you, the harder it is to get good bracing leverage. It's like trying to do a chin-up with your arms completely straight—the leverage just isn't there.

The High Brace

The high brace differs from the low brace in one fundamental respect: the elbows are held below the paddle shaft, instead of above. This puts the power face, not the nonpower face, in contact with the water. Because the elbows are below the paddle, the paddle is held higher than for the low brace, which makes it somewhat difficult to get the blade flat on the surface. This causes the high brace to be initially less effective than a low brace. The high brace's main advantage is that it provides stability over a greater range of boat angles. In fact, with a good hip snap, you can roll up on a high

HIGH BRACE

The high brace is similar to the low brace except that the power face is down and the elbows are below the shaft. You can easily convert a high brace into just about any other stroke.

brace. And the high brace is quick to place in the water, often faster than the low brace, because your hands and body are usually already close to being in high-brace position when you're paddling. Most strokes are easily changed into a high brace, and the high brace itself can be conveniently converted into a duffek, a forward stroke, or even a roll.

KEEP THE HIGH BRACE LOW. Although it seems contradictory, the proper high brace should be kept as low as possible; your top hand should stay below your chin. This makes your brace more powerful because the blade is nearly flat on the water. A low top hand allows you to avoid putting your arm in a vulnerable position above or behind your head, which can lead to shoulder strain or even dislocation. As with any brace, keep the shaft close to your body for the most effective use of your strength.

The Sweeping Brace

Most braces are done by placing the blade out to the side, then pulling it toward the cockpit and out of the water. In addition, both the low brace and the high brace can be swept across the water in a single motion, like a sweep stroke, but with the blade relatively flat on the surface. A sweeping brace is very effective because the blade covers a large area and gives a corresponding amount of support. As long as the blade is moving across the water, it won't sink. Anatomically, it's easiest to do a sweeping low brace from your stern forward. A sweeping high brace works best if you place it in one of the front quadrants and sweep back.

Do the sweeping brace by arcing the paddle out

As the blade moves across the water, its angle determines whether it will dive under or plane on the surface. For all recovery and rolling maneuvers, a climbing angle is needed.

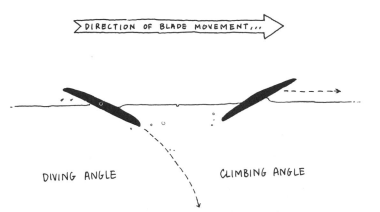

DIRECTION OF BLADE MOVEMENT

DIVING ANGLE   CLIMBING ANGLE

with your sweep arm while keeping the other arm tucked close to your chest. The nonsweeping hand thus acts like a fulcrum, and the paddle pivots at the point made by your inside hand. Do not push diagonally across your chest with your nonsweep arm or you'll do more of a sweep than a brace. This can be a hard habit to break completely, since most paddlers learn the forward sweep stroke first and get that pushing motion ingrained in them.

CLIMBING AND DIVING BLADE ANGLES. When sweeping while bracing, always maintain a "climbing" angle to the blade. If the forward edge (relative to the direction of movement) is angled up, the blade will remain on the surface. If the blade is angled down, however, the paddle will dive and you'll probably go diving in after it. A climbing angle to the direction of your sweep is important, but too much angle will divert energy into driving the boat either forward or backward instead of giving you a platform for the hip snap.

SCULLING. Sculling is a series of continuous high-brace forward and reverse sweeps in which the blade angle is switched to a climbing angle every time it changes direction. Sculling is a valuable maneuver that allows you to brace over a period of time. It's made considerably easier by keeping your head down. The motion of the scull is just like that of the drawing-while-feathering maneuver except the paddle is more horizontal than vertical and the boat is somewhat tipped.

PRACTICING BRACES. Playing Bronco Billy is a great way to practice your braces in flat water. Get in your boat and have a friend stand behind you in waist-deep water. Your friend will attempt to flip you by grabbing the back deck and twisting it randomly one way, and then the other.

The surprise element is important, so the flipping motions should be random. Start out slow and then speed it up. As the bronco rider, make sure your blade is always flat on the surface, not vertical, otherwise you'll be flipped in an instant. Be careful not to hit your friend with the paddle. Try both high and low braces, noticing the greater initial stability provided by the low brace. When high bracing, remember to keep your arms as low as possible for stability.

COMBINING THE HIGH BRACE AND THE DUFFEK. For novice paddlers, the duffek initially feels unsteady, since it doesn't provide you with any bracelike support. To alleviate some unsteadiness, practice the duffek with a slightly lowered top arm. This lowering places your blade somewhat parallel to the surface; you gain some support and are still able to turn your boat. As you gain balance and confidence, raise your upper arm to your forehead, the optimal duffek position, to get the blade vertical. The duffek–brace is a good stroke for beginners to use with eddy turns and peel-outs.

Rolling

The roll looks like one of the most glamorous and complex kayaking maneuvers, but in fact it's fairly easy to do. A solid, reliable roll will give you a lot of confidence on the river, confidence you need to try new river techniques without anxiety.

There are many styles of rolls. It doesn't really matter which one you do, as long as it's safe, reliable, and fairly quick. The body motions used to roll a boat upright are basically the same as those used to do the high brace, but you start off underwater.

MAKING IT EASY. The first rule of rolling is to stay calm underwater. You can then focus on learning to roll without panicking and thrashing your way out of the boat as soon as you go upside down. If you can hold your breath for a minute on land, you can certainly do it for 15 seconds underwater. Nose clips help with the initial learning process, but after you get a reliable roll, you'll be able to blow enough air out your nose to avoid a nasal douche. A face mask is also good to learn with on flat water. If you have the opportunity to practice in a pool or a warm, clear lake, so much the better. Wear enough insulation to stay warm—you want to be able to think clearly and enjoy the experience.

GENERAL ROLLING SUGGESTIONS. Strive for smooth, fluid motions. You can achieve smoothness by coordinating all your motions so that each one contributes its part to the roll. Coordinating the parts of the roll keeps you from having to muscle your way up with only your arms. A solid, smooth hip snap will help your roll considerably. The fact that a roll can even be done without paddle or hands attests to the importance of the hip snap in this maneuver.

Take it slowly when learning to roll. Trying to roll too fast is perhaps the biggest reason that rolls fail. Better to do one good—albeit slow—roll on the river than three feeble and rushed attempts.

As your rolling ability improves, you can speed it up for a fast, effective roll on white water. Once you get the roll on one side, work on the other; the ability to roll on both sides will give you maximum freedom. Also, watching a good "role" model will help you learn the roll quickly. For some whitewater rolling suggestions, see the end of the chapter.

THE IMPORTANCE OF KEEPING YOUR HEAD UNDERWATER. The most common problem for a novice roller is bringing the head up too soon. Your boat comes up halfway but then tips back over because your head rockets up. Subconsciously, your body is telling you that success depends on getting your head out of the water to breathe. The desire for oxygen is powerful. But this instinct is precisely the one you have to control. It's better to keep your head underwater for an additional second or two than to go for a whitewater swim.

As long as your head and upper body are in the

water (especially in white water with a PFD on), their buoyancy contributes to lifting the boat. As soon as you lift them out to get your breath of air, you become a lever arm that torques your boat back into the water. Trying to lift all your upper-body weight using only the resistance of the water on your paddle blade requires a superhuman effort. If you wait until the boat is nearly righted, however, then it's easy for your torso and head to follow.

Another way to describe the advantage of keeping your head down is in terms of angular momentum: once something starts moving around its axis, it won't stop unless acted upon by an opposing force. Thus, once the boat starts rolling back up, your body will follow suit. You don't want the weight of your upper body to provide an opposing force.

To reiterate: always, always, keep your head underwater until the boat is almost completely up. This can't be overemphasized. Really. If this continues to be a problem for you (as it is for many), try putting your head against your sweep arm's shoulder and keeping it there throughout all phases of your roll. You can even try biting your life jacket collar on that same side. If it's still in your teeth when you come up, you're keeping your head down.

The Sweep Roll

The sweep roll is very similar to a sweeping high brace, but the resistance of the water actually provides little support if you do the roll correctly; the timing of your body's movements is the main reason the roll works. It's convenient to separate the sweep roll into several distinct stages: the setup, the sweep, and the resurrection.

THE SETUP. For clarity, the roll will be described with the control hand forward in the setup position. First, lean forward against the deck. When you're upside down, you're in a good position to start your sweep. This position also minimizes your chances of hitting river-bottom rocks. In fact, if you're tightly tucked forward, the deepest part of you will be your life-jacketed upper back—and this will be only about 1½ feet below the surface.

Maintaining your proper paddle-grip position, place the paddle parallel to the boat, at the water's

The roll setup. This is the position to assume, whether rightside up or upside down. Notice that the sweep, or control, blade is power face up and flat on the water. The paddle is on the surface and parallel to the boat. The paddler is leaning forward. You should never change the control grip to attain the setup.

surface. The control (forward) blade needs to be flat on the water, with the power face up. To get this blade setting, you'll have to cock your control wrist somewhat in—a little awkward at first, but you can do it. Now you're ready to flip over.

As you tip, maintain your forward tuck and the paddle's position against, and parallel to, the boat. Don't allow the paddle to drift away from the boat or under the surface. As soon as the boat is completely upside down, notice that the paddle is on the surface and the power face is now aimed down toward the pool or river bottom—the correct placement for the roll. You're ready to initiate your sweep.

THE SWEEP. The sweep is tricky because it requires the coordination of several movements, including a sweep, a hip snap, and a front-to-back body motion. Remember, in this description the control arm is the sweep arm, and the other arm is called the inside arm (because it lies between your sweep arm and the boat.)

Okay, you're upside down and the paddle is on the surface, power face down, still parallel and next to the boat. Right before you begin the sweep, push up (skyward) with both arms to get the paddle a few inches above the surface; this will ensure that the paddle is indeed at the surface. Don't straighten your inside arm completely or the sweep blade will dive beneath the surface. But if you don't push up with it somewhat, the back blade will hit against the side of your boat, inhibiting your paddle from sweeping. Now start the sweep, getting as wide an arc as possible. Make sure you sweep the front blade away from the bow—there are few things more impossible than trying to roll up on one side but sweeping with the paddle on the other. This situation, believe it or not, is a common early mistake. Keep the blade sweeping on the surface because if it dives, your body will tend to dive with it. Keep your blade on the surface by employing three techniques: push your sweep arm upward, get a climbing angle to the blade (by slightly cocking your wrist in), and keep your inside arm slightly bent and next to the boat's side.

At the same time that you initiate your sweep, also begin your hip snap. Make it a long, drawn-out, and fluid hip snap; the term *hip snap* is somewhat of a misnomer when you are doing the sweep roll because the snap is really very mild mannered. Don't snap percussively, but rather synchronize it evenly with the sweep; start your hip snap as you start your sweep and finish them together. As you snap, you'll also be coming out of the tuck.

While all this is happening, watch the blade so that your head and torso follow its path. Also, make sure you maintain the current climbing angle. As your torso follows the arc of the blade, your body will uncurl from its tucked position to a position off to the side of the boat. Keep your head under. It's a lot to remember.

THE RESURRECTION. At this point, your hip snap is almost finished, the paddle is at a 90-degree angle to the boat, and the boat is nearly upright. The paddle should still be on the surface, and as long as your head is still under, you're 95 percent of the way there. You may need to push down on your paddle to get some support from the water (a brace), although the better you synchronize all the factors previously described, the less you'll need this extra bit of push. As you come up, your inside arm should be cocked, with the hand next to the shoulder. Come up leaning back on the deck. The farther you lean back on the deck, the easier the boat will come up because you're closer to the boat's axis of rotation. Voilá! Once again,

The same position as before, but upside down. Note that the entire paddle is out of the water. The boater is still leaning forward.

A split second later. The sweep arcs away from the bow and remains close to the surface. Notice that the arm closest to the boat, the left arm, is higher than the sweep arm. This lets the back blade slide over the hull and allows the sweep to travel in an unimpeded arc. If the left arm were completely straightened, the paddle would dive, precluding a roll.

do not rocket your head upright as you start coming up—even if you're sure that you're safe.

COMMON ROLL MISTAKES. Bringing the head out too soon is definitely the dubious winner in this category, but a close second place goes to paddle diving. Paddle diving occurs for three reasons: the inside arm extends up or away from the boat, the sweep arm pulls straight down instead of sweeping across the surface, and the paddle has a diving angle rather than a climbing angle. Always keep your inside arm next to the boat and slightly bent until you're completely upright. Don't push your inside arm across your chest as

The resurrection. The sweep has traveled back and the boater has gone from bending forward to leaning against the back deck. His left arm bends, and his right arm straightens. His head and body are at the same level.

Up. Notice that the left arm is bent and close to the torso.

you would in a forward sweep stroke. Use that arm as a stationary pivot point around which the paddle sweeps. Throughout the entire roll, your inside arm actually moves very little. In fact, it basically stays in place (relative to the outside world) and your body comes upright to greet it. You're using your inside arm correctly if, when you come up, your inside hand is against the corresponding shoulder. To keep your sweep arm from pulling your blade down, you may have to push up with the sweep arm to keep the blade on the surface; if you move your body correctly, you'll come up without having to exert much downward force on your blade.

The Hip-Snap Roll

The hip-snap roll is closely related to the sweep roll, with a few minor differences. It may be a bit harder to learn than the sweep roll, but some say it's slightly safer because the front of your body isn't left in a vulnerable position on the back deck if a first attempt fails. Remember, when you're tucked forward, you're most protected from river-rocks.

The setup is the same as for the sweep roll, and the paddle is then swept to a position 90 degrees to the

The hip-snap roll. The setup and initial stages are the same as for the sweep roll. Notice that the left arm is bent and the sweep blade is only just under the surface.

When the paddle is perpendicular to the boat, execute a powerful, side-to-side hip snap. The sweep blade acts as support and the head remains at or under the surface.

boat's side. Don't start your hip snap yet. Bend sideways at the waist to get your head near the surface (but of course, still under) and then do your hip snap. Unlike the sweep roll's hip snap, this snap should be done quickly—almost violently. Try to keep the blade flat on the surface when doing the hip snap. As always, keep your head down until the boat is completely up. The hip-snap roll is a bit more mechanical than the sweep roll because it consists of a two-part sequence rather than a single smooth motion.

The head is still angled down into the water. Even at this late stage, lifting his head would cause the boater to flip back under.

Only when the boat is completely upright can he raise his head.

The Extended Paddle Roll

The extended paddle roll (also called the Pawlata roll) can be done with either a sweep or a hip-snap roll format. The only difference in the setup is that your inside hand grabs the outside of the blade at the corner nearest the water's surface and the sweep hand moves toward the midpoint of the shaft to gain additional leverage. This roll is somewhat outdated (at one time this was the most commonly taught roll), but it is a good choice for those having difficulty learning to roll. Once mastered, the extended paddle roll is a good lead-in to the sweep or hip-snap roll. The transition is relatively easy, so the extended paddle roll should be used only as a temporary crutch.

The extended sweep provides tremendous leverage. Also, the inside hand position keeps you from having to worry about getting the back blade over the hull. On the flip side (pun intended), it's unwieldy and time-consuming to move your hands into position underwater and then back again once you're up. On the river, you usually want to roll as fast as possible.

The Hands Roll

This is a great maneuver if you've lost your paddle or you want to indulge in river play using hands-only skills. The hands roll isn't as difficult as it seems: a willingness to try is most of the battle.

Instead of a paddle, start by using a life jacket or a paddle board to roll. After a few successes, move on to a pair of hand paddles. The trick, with or without hand paddles, is to reach out to the side, keeping both hands together and above the surface. Maintaining them at the surface is the hardest part; you'll really have to bend sideways at the waist and stretch your arms upward. From this position, quickly slap the surface while simultaneously leaning back toward the back deck and doing a sudden, powerful hip snap. The head, as always, comes out last. With the paddle roll, you can sometimes cheat just a little and bring your head out sooner; with the hands roll, you can't. When you achieve more proficiency at hand rolling, you won't need to lean back much, but it helps at first.

For an additional challenge, try rolling your boat with only one hand.

The back roll is great for squirt and play paddling, which call for lots of flips in convoluted positions. Basically, all you do is set up with your sweep paddle at your stern and sweep the blade toward the bow. This skill is worth adding to your repertoire since it is often faster than setting up for a conventional roll if your blade is already behind you when you flip.

To practice the back roll, set up in the usual position. Now, maintaining the same relative positions of arms, paddle, and torso, lie back against your deck. Your sweep hand is now on your opposite shoulder and your inside arm is the arm nearest the bow. The blade next to your ear is power face up. Yes, it feels incredibly awkward. Now flip, maintaining this horrible position. It'll feel fine underwater. Really. Sweep the blade—power face down—from the stern to the side. You can either initiate a smooth, fluid hip snap at the same time you start your sweep, or wait until the paddle is at a 90-degree angle with the side of the boat to do a more powerful and sudden snap. Try to keep the blade on the surface. As long as your head stays down, you'll roll up in a high-brace position, but leaning forward. You can also do this roll by setting up with the power face down if you want to come up on a low brace.

The Back Roll

Usually you want to roll up as quickly as possible in white water, but there are a few occasions when waiting is wise. If your roll is borderline, slow down a little. Make sure your setup and movements are correct. A conscientious roll is usually successful on the first attempt, unlike a rushed one. It's always better to do one solid, slow roll than to do several energy-draining failures. If your first attempt is unsuccessful, set up again, and remember to keep your head down this time. Unless you think you could get caught on some rocks, it's better to hang in there and try several rolls than it is to swim.

THE UPSTREAM ROLL. All else being equal, it's easier to roll up on your downstream side. A downstream roll is aided by water moving under the blade, which helps keep it on the surface. If circumstances or

Whitewater Rolling Strategies

roll proficiency on only one side mandate an upstream roll, then wait a second or two to allow the boat to attain the same speed as the current—you're now effectively rolling in flat water. By waiting, you ensure that the blade won't dive and the upstream edge of the boat won't tip back upstream.

ROLLING IN WAVE TRAINS. If you're rolling in standing waves—especially if they're big—you'll want to time your roll so that you come up on the downstream side of a wave. The rationale is that if you roll up near the wave's peak, the support water under the blade will suddenly disappear, or you'll be hit by a wave's backwash and sent underwater again. The bigger the waves are, the more noticeable this effect. To time it right, wait underwater until you feel the boat bob up on the wave's peak, then roll up. This will also put you in position to brace into a downstream crashing wave, if there is one.

ROLLING IN TURBULENCE. If you're on a turbulent eddyline or near the backwash of a hole it's sometimes best to wait for things to calm down a bit before attempting a roll. Being under water in a tumultuous area can thoroughly disorient you, and often it's best to hang out until the water's power fades. Also, you could get lucky. It's extremely rare, but on occasion the river actually rights a tipped boater.

If you're set up on one side but the currents flips your boat partially back up on the opposite side of your setup (necessitating an impossible 270-degree roll rather than a 180-degree one), you'll need to do a hip snap to roll the boat completely upside down, odd as it may seem. Then you'll be able to do a normal roll.

FIVE

Reading White Water

LEARNING HOW TO READ WATER is like learning a foreign language. Just as being relaxed and confident helps your cross-cultural communication skills, being relaxed will also enable you to pick the best routes through rapids while in your boat. A cool head allows you to see clearly obstacles, drops, and paths, whereas anxiety clouds your vision so that you see only an undecipherable mass of white froth.

You would be wise to start off running rapids that are easy to decipher. All paddlers, regardless of skill, should get out of their boats and scout any section of water that lacks a clear route through it. When you scout from shore, remember that a rapid always looks different from upstream, in the boat. Identify clear landmarks (watermarks in this case) that you can easily spot from your boat. As you walk back upstream after scouting stop periodically to note the changing appearance of your selected watermarks.

To avoid confusion, be consistent in your use of directions on a river. The terms *left* and *right* are always used from the perspective of facing downstream. Thus, when looking upstream, *river left* refers to those features on your right.

White Water Morphology

The volume of water, steepness of gradient, profile of the river bottom, and type and shape of obstacles all contribute to the formation of a rapid's personality. Water is also moving beneath the surface in ways that are not always readily apparent on the surface. It can take some detective work to see all the paths and pitfalls.

VOLUME. Volume is the amount of water flowing past a point in the river per unit of time. In the United States, volume is almost always expressed in cubic feet per second (cfs), though occasionally it is given in some other dimension, such as cubic meters per second or cubic yards per minute. Depth gauges usually give the river level in feet, which is meaningful only if you know the individual river and therefore have a reference level or some other basis for understanding the relevance of the gauge reading.

A river's power and speed always increase with an increase in volume. This usually means a difficult river will become harder with more water, but sometimes the opposite is the case. Sometimes high water causes a rapid to wash out and diminish in intensity. Experience on a particular river is really the key to knowing what to expect.

High water can create other problems. Flooding can cause trees to fall into the river or be picked up from the banks, increasing the danger to boaters. Extremely high water also tends to wash out most of a river's eddies, those still-water havens behind rocks that are used for scouting and resting. On a difficult, flooded river, there's little room for error. The water can be so powerful that your strongest attempts at maneuvering will be ineffective. If you want to learn all sorts of fun facts about rivers in flood, see William Nealy's book, *Kayak*.

GRADIENT. River gradient refers to the average steepness of the riverbed. A rapid forms when a stretch of river has a higher gradient than the river's average. A consistently steep river forms one very long rapid. Conversely, pools form where the incline levels out and the velocity of the water decreases. Most rivers are characterized as pool-drop rivers, with the riverbed alternating between relatively steep, sections and level sections. These are the type of rivers most commonly run because they allow kayakers to rest after each rapid and provide them with an opportunity for checking out upcoming drops.

Gradient is measured in feet per mile. The most popular stretches for river running have gradients ranging from 10 to 100 feet per mile. The relation between gradient and difficulty depends, of course, on the individual river. Some rivers drop so evenly that they have miles of continuous low-grade riffles, despite high gradients. Conversely, a river with a low gradient may have miles of flat water with only one drop—a 200-foot waterfall.

As an extremely rough rule of thumb, most rivers that have gradients from 5 to 30 are usually Class I to II rivers, and gradients from 30 to 60 are likely to be Class III or IV (river classifications appear at the end of this chapter). But as always, this depends on the particular river. Rivers with gradients up to 300 feet per mile are run, but only by experts, crazed maniacs, or those who can't read topographical maps.

WATER VELOCITY. Water velocity depends on where it's being measured. In a straight section of river, the fastest current is in the middle where the river is deepest. Water velocity decreases toward the banks and near the river bottom. Friction accounts for much of this loss of speed.

STRAIGHT RIVER

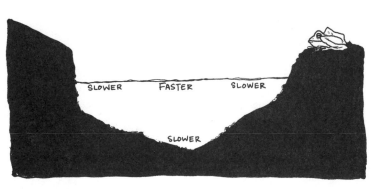

SLOWER   FASTER   SLOWER

SLOWER

In a straight section of river, the fastest water will be in midcurrent. Because of friction, water velocity will be slower where it is shallower as long as the gradient remains constant.

Water speed is fastest on a bend's outside, where the river is deepest.

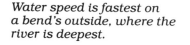

RIVER BEND

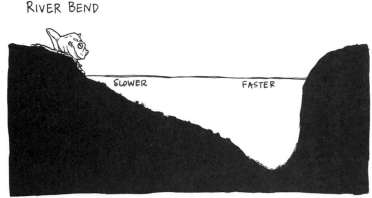

SLOWER   FASTER

When a river bends, a majority of the water travels on the outside of the bend. This causes a deeper and faster channel to form on the bend's outer curve. Because the inside of the bend has slower-moving water, not much of a channel is cut into the river bottom and the water is shallow. Often, the riverbank is higher on the bend's outside. If there are waves going around a bend, then the biggest and best waves are where the water is deepest—toward the outer bank. But be wary. The faster water at the outside of the turn can undercut the outer bank, causing trees to topple into the water. In addition, the outside bank may be covered with overhanging brush. The water wants to take you

Water velocity increases downstream and to the side of an obstacle. This is because water piles up above the obstacle and then accelerates as it flows past.

WATER SPEED INCREASES PAST OBSTACLE AND NEAR EDDYLINE

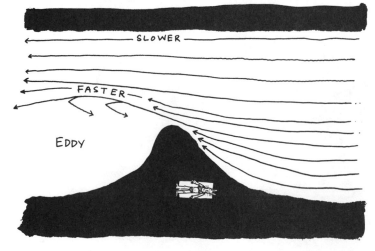

SLOWER

FASTER

EDDY

there, but this is not where you want to go, unless you enjoy being slapped and snagged by shrubbery.

When water hits an obstacle (midstream rock, bank outcropping, and so on), it piles up on the upstream side of the obstruction and then accelerates as it continues downstream. Consequently, water speed is somewhat faster downstream and to the side of (but not behind) any solid obstacle.

Waves

Waves are formed when water suddenly drops over an obstacle or a ledge. At these sites, water moving at a relatively high speed collides with slower water; energy is conserved in the form of waves. Waves are of three main types: standing waves, haystacks, and stoppers.

STANDING WAVES. Standing waves are the most common type found on rivers, and their consistent shape makes for great river playing. They're most often found in wave trains, a series of waves that diminish in size as the water moves downstream. They stay in place while the current flows through them, unlike ocean waves, which actually move through water that remains in place. For a boater the effect is largely the same.

Standing waves are usually perpendicular to the current, but sometimes they are diagonal in position. Diagonal waves are usually caused by diagonal rocks or ledges. A diagonal wave is almost always the first or

STANDING WAVES

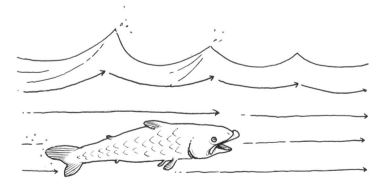

Standing waves are usually found in a wave train, a series of waves that decrease in size as they travel downstream.

When a wave gets steep enough, it crashes back on itself and a stopper is formed.

STOPPER WAVE

second wave in the train, but farther down the train the waves become regular, perpendicular standing waves. Diagonal waves are sometimes found on either or both sides of a tongue or chute. When diagonal waves are formed on each side of a chute, they converge downstream to give a V shape. At this convergence there is often a hole or stopper—a big wave that crashes back on itself. Big converging diagonal waves can funnel a boater into the hole.

HAYSTACKS. Haystacks resemble standing waves but are more peaked. They tend to move around (upstream, downstream, and side to side) and therefore are difficult to surf and play on. Haystacks are formed when several currents, coming from slightly different angles, merge. The standing waves of each current come together: some waves are in phase and augment each other, while others are out of phase and cancel each other out.

STOPPERS. An extremely steep wave falls back upstream on itself for the same reason that an ocean wave crashes, creating a wave with the characteristics of both a wave and a hole. These stoppers can abruptly halt an oncoming boater, but they also make great play spots where a skilled paddler can side surf, spin, and perform enders (see Chapter Seven) without getting terminally stuck.

A wave that curls back upstream but doesn't have quite the power of a stopper is called a curling wave. Curling waves are often positioned diagonally.

In most cases, the safest and easiest line through a rapid is where the water is fastest and deepest. This is also where the water generally forms a safe channel, free of obstacles. In paddling lingo, these channels are called by several names. Jets are especially fast sections of current. They are also called Vs or tongues for obvious reasons; the tip of the V points downstream. Chutes and Vs are found at the entrances to rapids and in the spaces between rocks. The V appears smooth if the water is slow and fairly deep, but is harder to see and can look like a bunch of peaking waves when the water is fast and turbulent. A chute is often the start of a wave train, but wave trains can occur anywhere in a rapid. The most benign chutes trail off into a deep pool, but often they are found in the middle of a rapid, punctuated or terminated by some other river formation, such as a rock or a hole.

Channels, Tongues, Jets, Vs, and Chutes

Chutes are fast jets of water found in places where the river narrows.

A CHUTE

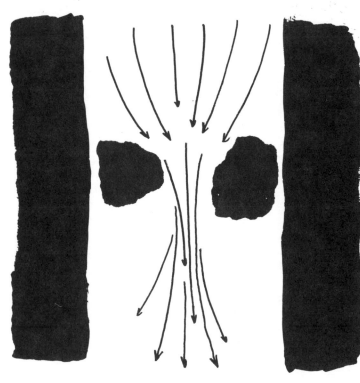

A fold, or crease, is often found where two currents meet. This area can be turbulent, especially if the currents are fast.

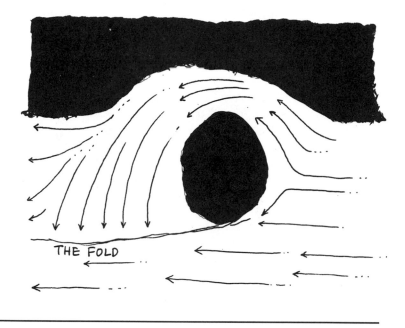

MERGING CURRENTS

THE FOLD

Converging Currents

When two currents converge, interesting things can occur through the various combinations of speed, volume, gradient, and converging angle. When the currents are flowing in approximately the same direction and their velocities are low, their mixing is gradual and fairly uneventful. But often one current is considerably stronger than the other. When this is the case, and the weaker current hits the stronger at something close to a 90-degree angle, some of the water from the weaker current folds under the stronger and some gets pushed up, above the level of the main flow. This fold, or crease, makes for an extremely turbulent area, especially if the river has a high-volume flow and the currents have a high velocity. Creases can be difficult places to paddle because they are so often full of whirlpools and surging, mixing currents.

Obstacles

Obstacles greatly determine the character of a rapid. Rocks are by far the most common obstacles, but logs, bridge pilings, and so on are also included. Unless otherwise stated, *rock* and *obstacle* are synonymous terms.

Water level influences what happens when water hits a rock. If the rock is above water, an area of slack current called an eddy forms behind the rock. If the water volume increases, water pours over the top of the rock, down the backside, and creates a depression in the slack water. This forms a feature known as a hole. If the level increases even more over the same rock, the hole is washed out and a series of waves forms. It's a fascinating process. Rivers in the eastern United States are good places to watch this hydrological transition, since many rivers are dammed and are turned on and off each day. Eddies, holes, and waves will be discussed in greater detail later.

Although rocks are responsible for many of the features that make rapids fun to run, they should be treated with respect. If you get sideways to one, you could become pinned on or around it. Chapter Six describes techniques for avoiding this. Be particularly cautious of sharp rocks formed naturally or by recent blasting in the area. Also, watch out for embedded

WATER LEVEL FLUCTUATIONS

During low flow, an eddy forms behind the rock. As the water level rises, the rock creates a hole, and finally, in very high water, a series of waves.

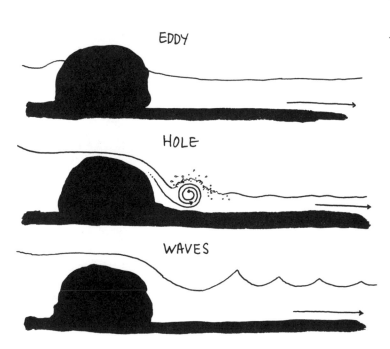

EDDY

HOLE

WAVES

steel rebar and pieces of sharp concrete from broken dams and bridges.

Rapids that are chock-full-o'-rocks are called *rock gardens.*

Logs and Strainers

Avoid them. A strainer is an obstruction that has water flowing through it, like a pile of logs or a single tree with its branches intact. They can hold you and add your boat to their collection of debris. These nasty obstacles are usually found upstream of islands, outside of bends, or pinned between rocks. But given the right conditions (right for the strainer, wrong for you), they can be found almost anywhere, so keep your eyes open. Be especially careful in the spring or after a storm, when high water has toppled new trees or re-arranged existing ones.

Watch for floating logs and debris, especially in flood. It's a nasty surprise to be surfing a wave and have a wooden behemoth crash down on top of you.

Undercuts and Potholes

Undercuts are places where the river has eroded its bank, leaving an overhang. During high water these undercuts may be completely submerged. Since the current goes through the undercut, a boater can, too. Undercuts are particularly dangerous when they harbor strainers. A boater can become wedged underwater, beneath the bank's outcropping—*not a good* scenario. Since you can't see below the water's surface, always assume that an undercut hides a strainer. When water hits a wall or an obstacle, it rises on it before continuing downstream (more on pillows and cushions in a moment). A lack of such a pillow can sometimes signify the presence of an undercut bank or rock.

← AN UNDERCUT

Undercuts can be dangerous, especially if water is covering them. A boater can get caught under one.

Potholes are most often found on geologically old rivers (like those in the Appalachians). They're formed by the spinning scouring action of pebbles trapped in small depressions. With time, these depressions can become fair-sized (a few feet in diameter) and can be 10 feet deep—large enough to trap a boater or a swimmer. Potholes are difficult or impossible to spot unless the water is low or clear. Avoid potholes for the same reason you avoid undercuts.

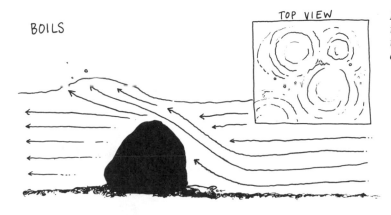

BOILS

TOP VIEW

Boils are formed when water rebounds off an obstacle, the river bottom, or a jet of current.

Boils

One kind of boil is caused by sitting in your boat too long. The other kind is formed when water hits the river bottom or an underwater obstacle and rebounds to the surface, pushing water above surface level. It actually looks like boiling water. You can make your own boils in your bathtub by pushing water up with your hand.

Boils are a common river phenomenon. They can indicate turbulent water, a shallow rock, or an undercut just upstream. Boils also occur where two currents merge. Some of the current is forced up, thus creating an upward surge of water. Powerfully boiling water isn't dangerous per se, but it can be unpredictable and difficult to navigate.

Pillows and Cushions

When water slams into an obstruction, it piles up on the upstream side, forming a mound of water called either a pillow or a cushion. A pillow is high on the upstream side of the rock and lower on the rock's sides, where it converges with the current. If the rock is above water, the cushion rises and then careens around each side. If the water level is high enough, the pillow goes over the top as well as around the sides. A hole is thus formed behind the rock. Pillows hiding submerged rocks can be detected from an upstream vantage point because the mounds will be somewhat higher than the surrounding current. Pillows can be welcome features because they act like force fields and help to nudge out-of-control boaters around rocks.

A pillow is the accumulation of water upstream of an obstacle. Water flows off the higher pillow and speeds up as it travels past the obstacle.

A PILLOW

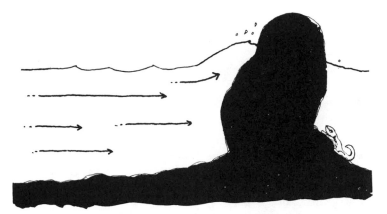

A CURLING PILLOW

Just as steep waves can fall back on themselves, so can pillows.

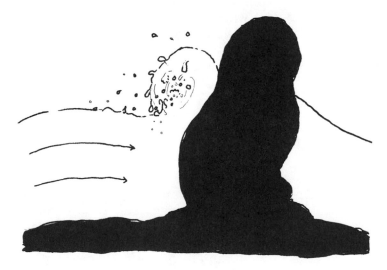

Big pillows can actually fall back on themselves, creating something like a stopper wave. They look intimidating but are usually fairly safe because of their huge bumper.

Eddies

An eddy is any spot in the river where the water is moving more slowly or in a different direction than the main current. Rocks in the river are the most common cause of eddies, but eddies also form behind logs, bridge pilings, and bedrock outcroppings, as well as on the inside of bends and along the riverbank where friction slows the water. The water in an eddy can move at a slower speed than the main current, be completely still, or most often, move back upstream. An eddy's character depends on the shape of the obstacle and on the level of the water. The faster the current is moving when it hits an obstacle, the stronger the current moving upstream behind the rock. This upstream current is always fastest just below the obstacle, making the eddy strongest near its top. The phenomenon of eddy water flowing counter to the direction of the main flow is caused by downstream water pulling eddy water downstream out the top of the eddy. Water from the downstream end of the eddy then moves upstream to fill the void. This leads to a constantly circulating flow of eddy water upstream and then down-

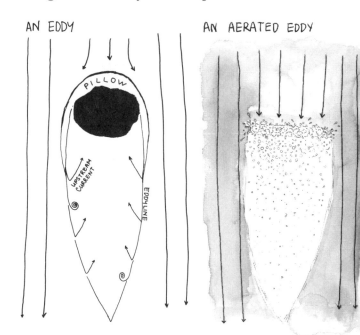

AN EDDY

PILLOW

UPSTREAM CURRENT

EDDYLINE

AN AERATED EDDY

Far left: Eddies are formed downstream of rocks. Sometimes the water is quiet behind a midcurrent rock, but usually it's moving upstream, opposite the direction of the main current. The eddyline forms the border between eddy and current and is a continuation of the upstream pillow. Whirlpools are formed on the eddy line by the opposing currents. **Left:** *A slightly submerged rock forms an aerated eddy. The eddy is white and frothy; the main current is dark by comparison.*

stream with the main current. A big powerful eddy on the side of the river with a lot of upstream current is, in essence, a giant whirlpool. The center is somewhat like the eye of a hurricane and is sunken in relation to the periphery.

DARK AND WHITE EDDIES. When the obstruction that causes the eddy is sticking out of the water, the eddy water is usually dark and unaerated. When water pours over the top of the obstacle, a hole forms, and the eddy water behind this hole is white because it's aerated. This aeration is caused by the mixing that occurs when moving water falls straight down into relatively still water. A white eddy is usually more turbulent than a dark one, although the eddy-current differential may not be as great.

Eddylines

An eddyline separates an eddy from the main current. Eddylines are usually sharpest and most distinct at their upstream end. They become less distinct farther downstream as eddy water gradually mixes with and assumes the same velocity as the main current. An eddy that is formed by an obstruction in fast current tends to have a fairly sharp and well-defined eddyline, whereas an eddy on an inside bend has an indistinct eddyline. A very large current differential makes for a strong eddyline. Eddylines also differ in their widths. A small eddyline can be crossed quickly, but a wide eddyline can be extremely difficult to navigate—it's loaded with boils, surging crosscurrents, and whirlpools.

WHIRLPOOLS. Whirlpools are caused by the shearing action of the current on the eddy water. They almost always occur on eddylines. Whirlpools on a river-right eddyline flow in a counterclockwise direction; river-left whirlpools circle clockwise.

EDDY FENCES. When extremely fast water hits a midstream rock, the resulting upstream pillow wraps around both sides of the rock as it continues downstream. Until the eddy peters out and merges with the main current, the current water is higher than the water in the eddy. The difference in height decreases as the eddyline moves downstream. This produces a sunken eddy, an eddy lower than the immediately surrounding current. The difference in velocity and height of this resulting eddyline can cause boaters some difficulty in exiting it smoothly, therefore earning it the label *eddy fence*, or *guardian eddyline*.

Rooster Tails

A rooster tail is a close relative of a pillow, but with an important difference. Rooster tails occur when extremely fast current hits a small rock that's close to the surface. Fast water hits the rock and sprays up into the air. Some people also refer to extremely peaked waves that have a plume of sorts as rooster tails.

Rooster tails are usually quite visible both from upstream and from shore. Look for them where the water is fastest—midway down a steep drop in the river, for example. Because they are indications of shallow, often sharp, rocks without cushioning pillows, avoid them.

There are two kinds of rooster tails: those formed by an obstacle that is pointed downstream, and those caused by an obstacle that is tilted upstream. Although it's good policy to avoid all rooster tails, the latter are the worse. The upstream angle of the rock can prevent a boat from riding over the rock, thus trapping it.

DOWNSTREAM-ANGLED PROTRUSION

UPSTREAM-ANGLED PROTRUSION

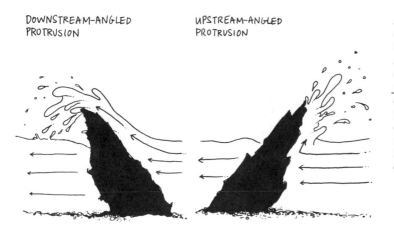

Far left: A rock pointed downstream in fast current will form a rooster tail of spraying water. It should be avoided, since the extremely fast water does not provide a cushioning pillow. Left: A rooster tail formed by a rock angled upstream in fast current. It is more dangerous to boaters than a downstream-oriented one.

Walls

A wall is a steep section of riverbank where the river runs into it head-on. Walls are often found on tight, twisty rivers. When current hits a wall, it should form a pillow proportional to the current's speed, volume, and angle of contact. A pillow that is smaller than expected could be a sign that the wall is undercut. Boiling water downstream can indicate the same hazard.

Holes, Reversals, and Hydraulics

When water flows over an obstruction, it hits the slack water downstream and creates an indentation, or a hole, as it plunges toward the bottom. Eddy water farther downstream of the rock is pulled upstream into this hole to replace the displaced water. The result is a circulating current that's pulled upstream, pushed down to the bottom, then back to the surface, and back upstream into the hole. Ad infinitum. The backwash is the frothy water that's flowing upstream into the hole. If the backwash is big enough, a boater's downstream momentum may be halted. The hole is like a vertical whirlpool. Many holes can hold a boat sideways because the force of the downstream current is equal to the force of the recirculating backwash. The boat is balanced between two essentially equal and opposite currents.

Holes go by many names, including reversals, hydraulics, souse-holes, and keepers. Some people maintain that there are differences among these terms, but in actual practice they are fairly synonymous. The ex-

A hole is made when water pouring over an obstacle punches the downstream surface. Downstream water, or backwash, flows back upstream to fill the hole. This area of recirculation is a fun place to frolic if the hole is safe, but not if the hole is a keeper.

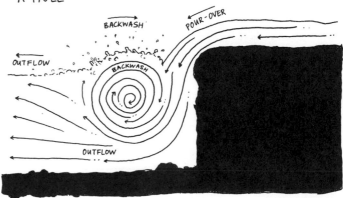

A HOLE

ception is the term *keeper*, which refers to a hole so big and nasty that a swimmer or boater would unwillingly stay in there for a long, long time. Keepers are dangerous because a swimmer gets recirculated along with the water and is pushed up to the surface for air once each cycle. In river slang, this is known as getting Maytaged. Even a small hole can hold a boat sideways. This can be fun if it's intentional (see Chapter Seven), but disconcerting if it's not.

Experience will guide you in deciding when a hole is dangerous and when it's fun. Steepness, depth, width, shape, and backwash length are all factors in determining a hole's personality.

DROP STEEPNESS. The steeper the drop, the greater the water velocity and the deeper it plunges below the surface. A steep drop can make for a nasty hole, even without the presence of a big backwash. When the water falls over the rock, it's called a pour-over. Pour-overs always form some kind of hole. If you're sideways in a hole formed by a steep pour-over, water coming over the drop can catch the upstream edge of your boat and flip you violently upstream. To avoid this, always lean the boat downstream. These steep holes may seem innocuous, but they are often the grabbiest: there's a lot of recirculation going on beneath the surface.

HOLE DEPTH. Hole depth is proportional to the speed and volume of water pouring over a ledge. A deep hole has more recirculating potential than a shallow one, and is therefore more dangerous. Holes that extend all the way down are especially dangerous because they can bounce you against the river bottom. A hole that reaches only partway down is usually safer because a swimmer isn't likely to get pummeled against the bottom before escaping.

If possible, check the depth of the water coming over the hole-forming rock; if it's too shallow, you could get clobbered by the rock if you flip upstream while sideways in the hole. The more water that flows over the rock, the safer the hole will be, all other factors aside.

A hole that extends to the river bottom can bounce a swimmer along the riverbed bottom.

WHOLE-DEPTH HOLE

A partial-depth hole allows the swimmer to escape in the outflow.

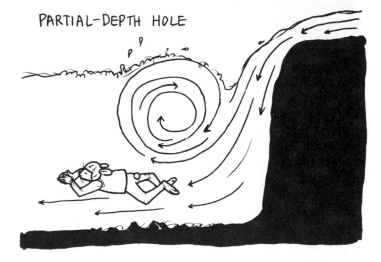

PARTIAL-DEPTH HOLE

HOLE SHAPE. The shapes of holes vary considerably, but the most common is the plain old generic hole that is straight and perpendicular to the current. Just like diagonal waves, diagonal holes are caused if the forming rock is long and diagonal to the current's flow.

Hole danger is usually measured by the degree of difficulty in getting out of a hole, and a simple visual test for this is the smile-or-frown rule. Look downstream. If the hole is smiling (its ends are downstream of its middle), you should be able to get out of it, since the best way to get out of a hole is to exit from one side,

HOLE SHAPES

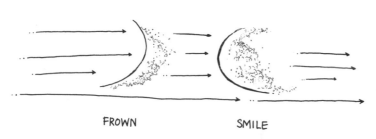

FROWN   SMILE

From upstream, determine whether a hole is frowning or smiling. Treat frowning holes with respect. Since it's easiest to exit holes from their ends, you would have to fight the current to exit a frowning hole. Smiling holes assist your exit by pushing your boat to a downstream end.

where the main current can help you. If the hole is frowning, beware! You'll be forced to travel upstream against the current to get out.

HOLE LENGTH. A hole's length is its measurement perpendicular to the current. In general, the easiest holes to exit are short and either straight or smiling. If the hole is frowning and shorter than a boat length, it can be hard to rock out (discussed in Chapter Seven). A long hole means you have to go farther to get out, and if it butts up against a bank, it may be impossible to exit. If both ends of the hole are hitting both sides of the riverbank, then you're really stuck. This

A LOW-HEAD DAM

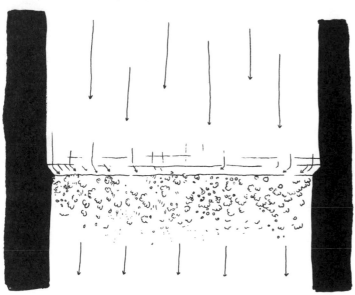

Low-head dams are extremely dangerous. The backwash of these dams tends to be considerable, even if the pour-over height is only a few feet and since they abut both shores, exiting out the ends is impossible.

explains why seemingly harmless low-head dams are so dangerous, even though they may drop only a few feet.

BACKWASH SIZE. The extent of a hole's downstream backwash can also determine how sticky it will be. The bigger the backwash, usually, the stickier the hole, but sometimes a small backwash will fool you and the hole will turn out to be sticky and deep. The farther downstream the backwash continues, the more difficult it is to get your boat over it, assuming you can't come out one side, the preferred extraction method. Backwash extending downstream more than a few feet may mean a nasty hole with tremendous recirculating power—another reason low-head dams are so dangerous.

Play paddlers often call backwash "pile" when they refer to a big fluffy backwash made from a hole good for playing in.

Waterfalls and Drops

When the river gradient increases to the point that water falls vertically, you have a waterfall. The term *drop* should, technically refer only to a waterfall, but it's often used to describe any rapid—regardless of difficulty. There is always some type of hole at the bottom of a steep drop, and its ability to hold a boater depends on all the factors influencing holes. Judge the difficulty of a drop not only by its height, but also by all the factors that make a hole safe or dangerous.

Waterfalls and steep drops come in a variety of sizes and shapes. They can be difficult to see while you're sitting in a boat because a horizon line creates a visual blending between the water above the ledge and the water below the waterfall. One of the best ways to spot a waterfall is by looking at the bank and observing whether the downstream scenery is significantly lower than the upstream scenery. Even this strategy is not foolproof, however. Rising mist or a telltale dull roar are unmistakable warning signals that a drop is ahead.

Currents that converge at the brink of a steep drop sometimes produce a vertical "fold." It's good policy to avoid a vertical fold because it can pull a boater into its crease like an eggbeater.

HORIZON LINE

Horizon lines can be nearly invisible. Watch carefully for them and scout if a safe route isn't apparent from the boat.

Beware of rooster tails midway down a steep drop, as well as rocks at the bottom. Boils that are exceptionally high above the surface of the bottom pool can indicate subsurface rocks. Never run a waterfall without knowing what's below it.

River Rating

A standard classification system exists for rating the difficulty of rapids and rivers. Class I water is the easiest water, and Class VI is the hardest and most dangerous. As with school grades, there are also plus and minus suffixes to distinguish difficulty within each class. Thus, a Class II+ run is slightly more difficult than a regular Class II river. And Class II water, in turn, is slightly harder than Class II– water.

Naturally, there's a lot of subjectivity in such a ranking system. Originally, the system combined both difficulty and other danger factors. For example, a river that was icy-cold and miles from the nearest road would be rated higher than a technically similar river that was tepid and only a mile from a hospital. Today the ratings tend to reflect only the rapid's pure technical difficulty. This trend, however, does not mean that extra-aquatic factors are irrelevant. You should always incorporate every outside factor into your decision of whether to run something. If you're deep in a remote gorge or tired from a long day, be more conservative about your route.

There's also a considerable amount of individual

interpretation. An expert boater may rate a river Class III, when to nearly everyone else it's obviously a hard IV stream. On the other hand, some paddlers glorify their exploits by overrating runs. With them, you may automatically have to subtract a full level of difficulty to get an "objective" rating. Learn whom to trust. Generally, as the population's paddling skills improve, ratings shift downward. Sections of rivers that 20 years ago were rated Class V are now rated Class III. Remember, too, that a river's rating can change as the water level fluctuates.

All in all, ratings provide only a rough estimate of the difficulty of a river. Take them with a grain of salt.

CLASS I. This is slow-moving water with few or no obstacles. Easy to read, easy to paddle.

CLASS II. The water is faster and the river makes a few bends. Rocks, holes, and waves are present but recognizable from upstream and easily avoided. Requires basic whitewater skills.

CLASS III. The current is faster yet, and rocks, waves, and holes increase in both number and size. Routes are fairly apparent, but shore scouting is advisable. A reliable roll is highly recommended. Your whitewater skills should be in good shape.

CLASS IV. The water is difficult, big, or both. Holes and waves may be quite big, and finding a clean route will require some detective skill. Should you get off-line, there's a possibility of getting trashed. Scouting is mandatory for all but the best paddlers. A solid roll is a necessity.

CLASS V. Class V water is, essentially, the upper limit of what can be run without serious risk, even by experts. Scouting is a must. The rapids are exceedingly complex or turbulent. Holes may be very large and nasty. You have to be "spot-on" to run Class V water. The price for not being exactly where you want to be can be high.

CLASS VI. Basically unrunnable. Niagara Falls, for example, qualifies quite admirably for a Class VI rating. Someone claiming to run Class VI water either is suicidal or, more likely, has overrated the water.

SIX

Whitewater Maneuvers

YOU'RE FLYING SMOOTHLY DOWN A FAST JET OF WATER past some house-sized rocks. Suddenly you whip into an eddy. You ferry across the current with one stroke and rocket into an eddy on the other side of the chute. Peeling out, you head downstream, zip across an eddy or two, then shoot down over a 2-foot drop into a deep, green pool.

This is the real stuff, where your judgment and technical abilities meet the river. River running is a complex skill, but knowing some rules will simplify things and help you get the feel of white water. Most river-running techniques are variations on a few key maneuvers, which you'll read about here. If you're already an experienced paddler, you'll find tips about how to improve your skills. But first, some basics about running rivers safely.

The Elements of Safety

Good judgment combined with a high skill level makes a dynamite combination. If, however, you lack some technical precision, common sense can make up for a lot. Pick the best route through a rapid rather than just blundering ahead. Or take the "sneak" route instead of the macho line. Portaging is always an option for a particular run that may not be worth the risk at your present skill level.

When deciding whether to run a rapid, take every factor into account: the difficulty of the rapid, your skill and confidence, air and water temperature, and the proximity of assistance. As you assess the difficulty of a rapid, consider the sharpness of the rocks, the presence of undercuts or strainers, and the length of the rapid. Also notice where the particularly challenging spots are. If the difficult area occurs just upstream of a long, deep pool, great. But if it's near the beginning of the rapid, you may be in for an unpleasant swim. Rivers that have continuous rapids should be run more cautiously than pool-drop rivers, since a longer swim out is possible. Never trap yourself in a spot from which you can't safely finish running the drop, out, or paddle upstream.

RIVER STRATEGIES. Your best safety strategy is to avoid anything even remotely dangerous. Ideal, impossible, and no fun. Sooner or later, you'll find yourself in a potentially dangerous situation no matter how conservative you are. What you need is a couple of general principles, based on the premise that your best defense is a good offense, to make paddling safe and still challenging. First, it's usually best to paddle somewhat aggressively downstream rather than drift through a rapid. If you're moving faster than the current, you have more control than if you let it carry you. Also, each time the paddle is in the water, you've got additional stability. Continuous paddling provides momentary pontoons on each side of your boat.

Second, lean into—or paddle aggressively through —anything that appears intimidating. Use finesse to avoid a nasty situation. But failing that, adopt a linebacking strategy. For this to work, you'll have to overcome a natural response to cringe and lean away from whatever appears frightening. Meet force with force.

Example One: If you're unable to avoid a big hole or a stopper wave, paddle hard and straight ahead in an attempt to punch straight through. Insert a forward stroke downstream of the backwash. This will help you pull yourself through the hole. If you passively drop into a hole, your bow will go down and the hole

HOLE PUNCHING

Paddling aggressively straight through a hole or stopper is the best way to keep it from stopping you.

will stop you, turn you sideways, and hold you. If you do hit a hole sideways instead of head-on, always lean aggressively downstream into the froth. Don't let your upstream edge get caught by water coming over the drop or you'll windowshade—a particularly violent upstream flip.

Example Two: If you're sideways and close enough to a rock that pinning or broaching your boat is a possibility, always, always lean your boat and body into the rock. You can even let go of your paddle and embrace the rock like an old friend. Then you can push yourself to wherever it's safe. Make sure you lean the boat downstream so that the current doesn't catch your upstream edge and flip you. If you followed your untrained instincts and leaned away from the rock, the boat would flip upstream, giving the current a chance to pin you and your boat against—or worse, around—the rock. If you don't like the idea of hugging a rock, practice drifting and leaning onto a rock in mild current.

LEANING INTO A ROCK

If hitting a rock sideways is unavoidable, lean your body onto the rock while leaning your boat downstream. This will prevent the boat from flipping and pinning on the rock. Push yourself off to one side using a free hand. This is one of the very few situations where letting go of the paddle with one hand is recommended.

One last suggestion. Whenever possible, keep the boat aligned parallel and downstream to the current. This gives you the most control and the best view of the river. A sideways boat tends to stick in holes, be slowed by waves, or pinned on rocks. If you can't go through a rapid pointed downstream, go backward. Running a rock-filled rapid sideways should always be your last choice.

SWIMMING OUT. Bailing out of your boat should be avoided unless you've flipped over and there's something really nasty just downstream. You have more options in your boat than you do out of it. Try as many good roll attempts as you can. But if they all fail, then you'll have to swim.

Lean forward as you push yourself out of your boat for the same reason you do when setting up for a roll: to avoid rocks. Extricate yourself with the same care you took getting into your boat; pop your sprayskirt and push yourself out. Attempting to exit your over-turned boat too fast is a bit like trying to pull your fingers quickly out of a Chinese fingercuff puzzle. Remember the Zen rule: less is more and slower is faster. Exiting slower allows a faster escape.

Once you're free of the boat, your natural tendency will be to try to stand up in the water. Don't. You could catch your foot on something and be held under-water by the current. Instead, assume the whitewater swimming position. You won't look like an Olympic

The whitewater swimming position: feet downstream and slightly bent. The idea is to keep your body as near to the surface as possible. Never attempt to stand unless the water is less than knee deep and moving slowly.

THE SWIMMING POSITION

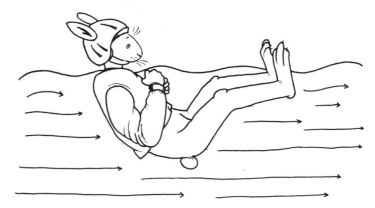

swimming champion in this position, but it is the safest one for white water.

The whitewater swimming position is achieved by simply lying on your back, with your feet together and pointed downstream. Keep your body and legs as close to the surface as possible. Your knees should be slightly bent to act as shock absorbers if you hit a rock. (If this happens, just push to one side of the rock, and float on downstream. Make sure you push yourself to the same side your boat goes, if it's a safe route.)

Once you're in the swimming position, reach for the grabloop on the upstream end of your kayak. Grab your paddle, if possible. Always hold on to the upstream end of the boat; you don't want to be caught between it and a rock, and you can better guide its direction from this position. Unless you're in serious danger, always hold on to your gear. You don't want to be stuck on the river without it. Keep your boat upside down to prevent additional water from splashing in. Also, when the boat is upside down, it traps a bubble of air, making it easier to pull toward shore since the air provides some flotation. Stay with your boat unless it's drifting into a nasty spot. Then, make like a rat and abandon ship.

If someone throws a rope to you, never attach yourself directly to it, not even by wrapping it around your arm. You want to be able to let go at a moment's notice. Hold on to it with a free hand and set your same elbow over it, so that the rope is firmly under your armpit. Keep the rope tightly between your arm and body until you reach the shore.

If you're on your own, stroke for shallow, slow water or an eddy; watch out for overhanging bushes and sharp rocks. It's easiest to hold your upstream grabloop and your paddle with the same hand so that you can stroke with your free arm. If you're being helped by a fellow paddler, this leaves a free hand to hold the rescuer's stern grabloop. When you're being towed to shore, help out by kicking. don't let your friend do all the work—it's amazingly difficult to haul a swimmer through the water. Don't attempt to stand up until you know the water is less than knee-deep and slow-moving enough to allow you solid footing.

SELF-RESCUE

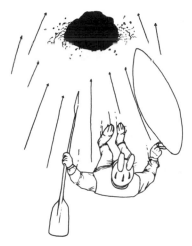

Until you get help or can negotiate to shore, maintain the swimming position through rapids. Keeping the boat upside down will provide flotation and prevent more water from entering. Bend your knees; they will act as shock absorbers if you bump into a rock. Stay on the same side of the rock as your boat, unless that route looks unsafe.

These are basic but extremely important safety tips. A thorough discussion of safety and of river rescue techniques would require a full-length book. Luckily it's already been written. *River Rescue,* by Les Bechdel and Slim Ray, should be a part of the library of anyone who paddles on rivers.

Now it's time to learn some of the bread-and-butter maneuvers used by kayakers on rivers: wave paddling, ferries, eddy turns, peel-outs, and S turns.

Paddling in Waves

All sorts of fun things can be done in waves: you can surf them, paddle through them, run them straight on. There are two ways you can run straight through a wave chain: through the middle of the waves, or along the eddyline. The kind of ride you get depends on the route you choose. If you take the ride through the center, you'll get a roller-coaster thrill, with lots of up and down bobbing and splashes at the tops, especially if the waves curl back upstream. Although this type of ride is the most fun when there's an easy washout or big pool below, the waves slow your boat and make it more difficult for you to stay in control. At the peak of a wave, both ends will be out of the water and the boat can spin very easily—sometimes too easily. If you're in the wave's trough, however, both ends will be submerged and the boat can be spun only with difficulty.

To stay in control or to remain dry, you want to choose a route just to the current side of the eddyline. Here the path is usually clear of obstacles and the waves are much smaller.

On a wave peak your boat has more effective rocker, so it spins easily.

TURNING ON A WAVE PEAK

TRAPPED BY WAVE PEAKS

It's not nearly so easy to spin in a wave's trough.

You can also run a wave train sideways (knowing, of course, that no mean holes lurk downstream). Be ready to brace downstream into the waves (especially if they're stoppers) and to balance as you ride over the peaks.

Ferries

Ferries are the maneuvers by which a paddler crosses from one side of the river to the other without being swept downstream. They are some of the most basic and useful river maneuvers. A ferry allows you to avoid something nasty downstream or get to a great play wave on the other side of the river with minimal effort. Besides, ferries are a blast; a snappy one across a fast jet of water can give you the sensation of flying.

Ferries work because of the relationship between two forces: the force of the current carrying you downstream and the force of your paddling at an upstream angle. You end up traveling in a direction dictated by the strength of each of these forces and the angle between them.

Ferries can be done with the bow pointing either upstream (the usual ferry position) or downstream (a back ferry). A ferry with your bow facing upstream is the easier of the two because forward strokes are more powerful than back strokes. It's also easier to judge your ferry angle relative to the current when you're facing upstream, so it's easier to make the appropriate adjustments.

Most ferries are done from an eddy into the current, and often the trickiest step is crossing the eddyline. Boat lean, ferry angle, and boat speed contribute to the effectiveness of this maneuver. These factors are

The ferry allows you to travel across the current without losing "ground." Angle upstream and paddle to counteract the current's force. The faster the current, the farther upstream you'll have to point and the harder you'll have to paddle.

THE FERRY

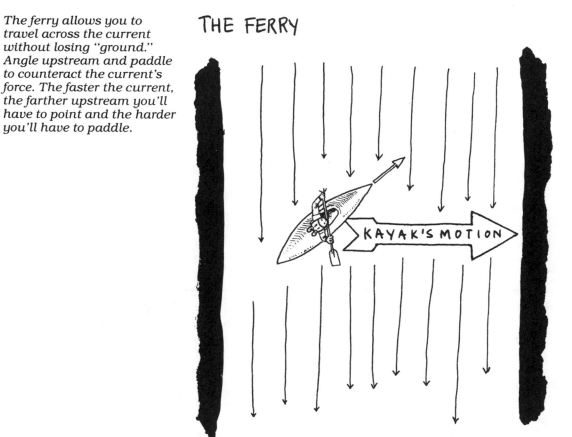

interrelated—how much you do of one depends on the strength of the others.

DOWNSTREAM BOAT LEAN. To keep the current from hitting your upstream edge and flipping you, lean the boat downstream slightly by lifting your upstream knee. This is basically a version of the hip snap described in Chapter Four. The downstream lean keeps you from flipping by keeping your upstream edge out of the water. When novices flip, 90 percent of the time it's because they don't lean the boat downstream as they come out of an eddy. Always remember to lean your boat more than your body. Also, lean just before your boat enters the current. Anticipate! If you wait until after boat and current meet, it may be too late. The faster the current, the more you'll need to lean downstream. When you're first learning to ferry, be conservative. Exaggerate your leans somewhat. Once you start getting the knack, tone down your lean to eliminate overkill. After you're past the eddy-line and are in the midst of a ferry, you can diminish your lean.

FERRY ANGLE. The correct ferry angle is critical because it minimizes your energy expenditure while maximizing the speed and efficiency of your ferry. It takes experience to recognize the correct angle, which depends on the speed of the current, your speed, and your desired destination. As a rule of thumb, exit most eddies with your boat pointed upstream at an angle of 45 degrees or less relative to the eddyline. If you're new to ferrying, choose an angle between 5 and 10 degrees. Later with experience, you can be less conservative and increase the angle. If the current is really slow, however, you can change the angle to 60 degrees or greater. When the current is riproaring, you'll need a very small angle; plan on pointing almost directly upstream as you ferry.

Besides being inefficient, an incorrect exit angle can foul up your ferry. Too wide an exit angle allows the oncoming water to hit the bow and push your boat downstream instead of across the river. This is a common beginner's problem. (When this is done intentionally, it's called a peel-out, which is discussed later in this chapter.) If the angle is too small, your boat may swing around and angle back into the eddy that you are attempting to leave. If you're in doubt as to the

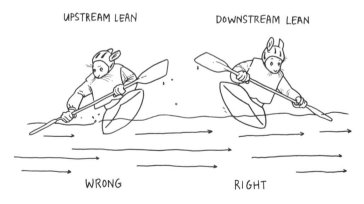

UPSTREAM LEAN   DOWNSTREAM LEAN

WRONG   RIGHT

When you exit an eddy into the current, always lean your boat downstream. If you lean upstream, the current will catch your upstream edge and flip you.

*The optimal ferry angle
depends on current and boat
speed. In general, keep it
between 10 and 45 degrees.
The faster the current, the
tighter the angle. You can set
a wider angle if you have a
lot of boat speed.*

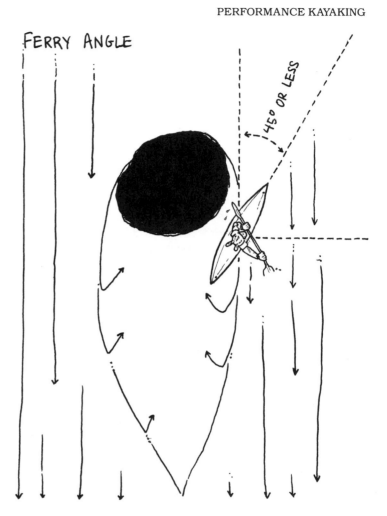

FERRY ANGLE

45° OR LESS

correct angle, err on the side of being pointed upstream. It's much easier to turn your boat downstream
if you don't have enough angle than it is to turn it
upstream if you have too much. You want to work with
the current, not against it.

BOAT SPEED. You'll need a good head of steam
to paddle up the eddy. The faster the current is, the
more speed you'll need. Match your speed with the
current's speed. If you have a broad angle, perpendicular to the current, you'll need more speed to keep your
bow from getting swept downstream. Don't put your
bow slowly and lazily out into the current. The current

will throw the bow downstream while the stern stays in place, held there by the eddy, and you'll do an out-of-control spin on the eddyline. Do a few solid forward strokes in the eddy to generate momentum before you hit the current.

STROKE TIMING AND PLACEMENT. The correct placement and timing of your last strokes as you leave the eddy will improve your ferry. Your last stroke (usually a forward stroke, but possibly a sweep if you need a last-minute angle adjustment) should be placed on your downstream side in either the eddy or the current. This stroke compensates for the force that the current imparts to the boat. Ideally, this final stroke comes into full force just as the current comes in contact with the bow, and both forces cancel, with the boat continuing on its original intended path. The exact amount of force to apply to your stroke varies depending on the situation—experience is the teacher here. Learn to anticipate the force trying to turn you downstream.

Avoid doing a forward stroke or sweep on your upstream side as you leave the eddy. If you intend to do one of these strokes to adjust your angle, fine. Some paddlers, however, are unaware they're making their exit stroke on the upstream side. They end up turning slightly downstream and losing their ferry angle before they even cross the eddyline.

THE ONE-STROKE FERRY. You can do a great ferry by placing a stern draw on your downstream side just as you leave the eddy. The stern draw doubles as the last corrective stroke and the stroke that ferries you across the current. If you have a lot of speed as you exit the eddy and you don't have to ferry too far, you can continue to pull on your stern draw. As long as your boat has speed, the current exerts force on your paddle and you move through the water. You're pulling against the water with your stern draw, but the blade remains in place. This stern draw is thus a static stroke because it remains in place, relative to the boat, even though both you and the water are exerting force on it to move the boat across the current. If you stop pulling on your stern draw and leave it in the water,

98 PERFORMANCE KAYAKING

Preparing for the ferry. The boater is in the eddy behind the rock; current is flowing from right to left. Notice that the boat is angled nearly upstream but with a very slight crosscurrent orientation. The paddler is gathering a head of steam in the eddy to compensate for the current.

Ferrying. The downstream lean facilitates the ferry and keeps the boater from flipping upstream. The boat angle is greater than it was in the previous picture because the force of the current on the bow has turned the boat slightly.

The ferry continued. The paddler is moving across the current without getting swept downstream. Notice that the paddler maintains a slight downstream lean.

The stern draw option. Instead of paddling with forward strokes, the boater has inserted a downstream stern draw to prevent the current from pushing the bow downstream. If conditions are right and you have enough boat speed, you can ferry across the entire river on this one stroke.

it functions like a rudder. With the rudder, you can maintain or adjust your ferry angle as you move across the current by moving the blade either away from or toward the stern.

WHERE TO EXIT. Some places are better than others for exiting the eddyline. The top of the eddy is usually the best spot, even though the water is a little faster there than farther downstream. The current near the top of the eddy usually produces fairly smooth, consistent water. There are fewer eddyline swirlies, so you can maintain your angle more easily. Downstream, it becomes more turbulent as current and eddy mix. In addition, many eddies tend to push you to their tops because of the upstream eddy current. Why fight the eddy's natural tendency? You may, however, need to take the eddy's upstream current into account if it is carrying you in the wrong direction for your exit. Compensate by adjusting your angle accordingly as you paddle up the eddy.

MAINTAINING YOUR FERRY. Once you have the correct ferry angle, just paddle forward to make your way across the river or chute. Remember that the speed of the current can vary across the width of a river, requiring you to adjust your ferry angle. To correct your ferry angle put in several hard forward strokes or a sweep. Maintaining your angle is pretty easy if you do a stern draw on your downstream side.

It may be tempting to do a backstroke on your upstream side to correct angle deviations. A backstroke *is* an effective means of correction, but it ends up slowing the boat so much that you may get pushed too far downstream.

Again, always err on the side of being pointed upstream, not only while exiting the eddy, but also while in midcurrent. It's easier to turn the bow downstream with the help of the current than upstream against the current.

ADVANCED FERRIES. When exiting an eddy with a ferry, always aim the bow into the trough of a wave so that you can surf the boat as you ferry (surfing is discussed in Chapter Seven). Try this technique even on small waves of only a few inches in height; the benefits are still noticeable and you'll get into the habit of exiting onto wave troughs. Surfing while ferrying allows you a broader ferry angle because gravity holds you in place. You can really whip across the current with this maneuver. This saves you a considerable amount of energy, since the wave helps to shoot you smoothly across the river. Always let the river do the work.

The wider your ferry angle is, the speedier and more efficient your ferry will be. If you're ferrying over to another eddy, it might be a good strategy to go perpendicular to the current so that you get a good entry angle across the second eddyline. If the current is too

Surfing a wave while you ferry will make your cross-current trip faster, easier, and more fun.

fast, however, you may not be able to make the broad angle without being swept downstream. It's up to you to find the right balance.

As you're exiting an eddy, try leaning back right before you hit the current. Leaning back causes your bow to come out of the water a little, preventing it from immediately reacting to the current's force. In strong current you can get away with a wider exit angle if you lift your bow at the same time that you place your final downstream stroke.

As you're ferrying, try paddling with only forward strokes. Avoid doing correctional sweeps. Also try experimenting with radical downstream leans as you ferry; if the current is fast and you have a lot of speed and a good angle, this can be a pratically quick way of ferrying because you present the current with a lot of hull area—it's like adding sail on a sailboat.

The Back Ferry

The back ferry is most commonly used to avoid obstacles and to move across the current while keeping the boat pointed downstream. It's one technique used to maneuver through rock gardens. The back ferry can be done from an eddy into the current, but it is also frequently used when you're already in the current, pointed and moving downstream.

THE MIDCURRENT BACK FERRY. To back ferry while in midcurrent, backpaddle a bit to slow or reverse the speed of the boat, and then do a small reverse sweep to set the appropriate ferry angle. Once the angle is set, backpaddle diagonally across the current. If your stern gets pushed downstream, it's extremely difficult to regain the correct angle, so be especially conservative. You may have to put in some back sweeps on your downstream side to keep your stern pointed upstream. If you lean forward a little when doing these reverse sweeps, the stern will lift slightly, making it a little easier for you to sweep the stern upstream.

THE EDDY-TO-CURRENT BACK FERRY. If the back ferry is being done from an eddy, keep the stern pointed almost directly upstream and be ready to put in some powerful, downstream, reverse sweep strokes to maintain your angle. Because you're paddling backward, it's difficult to get a lot of momentum across the eddyline; you'll have to compensate by setting a small angle. Finally, look over the shoulder that's nearest the current for a clear view of the eddyline so that you'll know when to do the necessary correction strokes.

Eddy Turns

Eddy turns are the staple of river paddling. They allow you to stop and rest, scout rapids from the boat, and maneuver through rapids. What's more, they're just plain fun. Rocketing into a powerful eddy with a fast, smooth turn is a great feeling, a little like nirvana.

An eddy turn works because the boat spins as it enters the eddy. The part of the bow that's in the eddy moves upstream or stays in place while the stern continues to be pushed downstream by the current. If you have the correct angle as you hit the eddyline, your forward speed converts the spin into an arcing turn; the greater the entry speed, the faster the eddy turn.

To do the eddy turn, you first need to get into the eddy. Then you can actually carry out your turn, adjusting its radius as you go. Like the ferry, the eddy turn depends primarily on the now-familiar components of lean, angle, and speed.

LEAN. When doing most eddy turns, lean your kayak (not your body) to the inside of the turn by lifting your downstream knee. If you lean to the outside, or downstream, as you hit the eddy, you'll flip or at least need to brace; it's just like leaning upstream when you come out of an eddy on a ferry. *Remember*: lean downstream when you come out of eddies and upstream when you come into them.

The trick to the lean is in the timing; you want to lean just as the eddy starts grabbing the bow. No sooner, no later. The greater the current differential and the greater your speed, the more you need to lean.

ANGLE. Your biggest task is to find the best angle between your boat and the eddyline. If you get this right and you have some speed, the turn occurs almost by itself, requiring little additional effort on your part. Your angle to the eddyline depends on the strength of

EDDY—TURN ANGLE

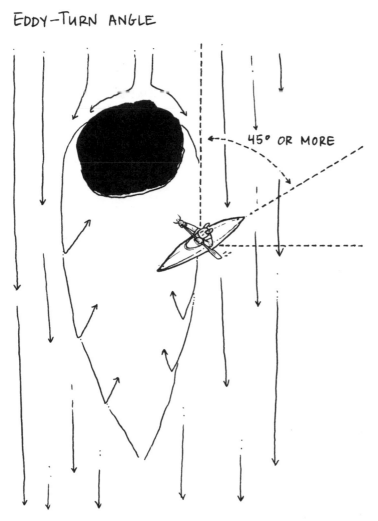

45° OR MORE

The ideal eddy turn entry angle is 45 degrees or more. The greater your speed, the wider the angle you can set. Lean the boat upstream, or into your turn, when entering an eddy.

the current, the power of the eddy, the width of the eddyline, and your speed. As a general rule, set the angle at 45 degrees or greater from the eddyline.

THE LAST STROKE. The type and placement of your last stroke depend on your angle. This is your last chance to correct the boat angle before meeting the eddyline. If you're parallel to the eddyline, you'll need to do a sweep or a forward stroke–sweep combination on the downstream side to set the correct angle. Don't do such a powerful sweep that you end up pointing somewhat upstream as you hit the eddyline. This will cause you to spin out before penetrating the eddy. On the other hand, you may need to decrease your approach angle by doing a sweep or forward stroke on your upstream side. Again avoid doing too powerful a stroke, or you may be deflected off the eddy-line and careen downstream.

If you do a sweep on your downstream side to set your angle, make sure you lean the boat to the inside of your turn as you enter the eddy. The timing of this lean is important because you usually do an outside lean when you sweep on your downstream side. In this case, however, you're set up for a downstream lean as soon as you hit the eddy, which can result in an incredibly quick, unintentional flip.

In big, turbulent water you'll often need to do one

The initiation of an eddy turn. Water is flowing from right to left. The boat is still in the current and a forward stroke-sweep is used to attain the correct eddy entry angle.

The right sweep is finished and the boat is now crossing the eddyline at a 45-degree angle. Notice how the boat is leaned upstream as it crosses the eddyline. The boater is about to insert a duffek stroke on his left in the eddy.

or more strong sweeps on your upstream side. The eddyline is so wide that a significant differential exists even before you get to the main eddy, and the boat tends to spin, bow upstream, before you get into the main part of the eddy.

SPEED. Your speed depends on your angle and vice versa. The more speed you have, the more perpendicular an angle to the eddyline you can get away with. If the eddy-current differential is small, you won't need a lot of momentum; it'll be easy to punch through the eddyline into the main part of the eddy. If you don't have much speed and the current differential is high, the eddy will have time to grab your bow while the

The boat is now deep in the eddy and is still being leaned upstream. The duffek has been inserted parallel to the boat and the boat is turning around the pivot point provided by the paddle. You can vary the tightness of the turn by pulling the blade toward the bow and adjusting the blade angle.

The boat is well in the eddy and pointed nearly upstream. Notice the continuing on-side lean.

EDDY ANATOMY

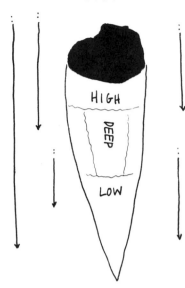

You'll get the best turns by aiming to place your boat both high and deep.

current continues to push your stern downstream. You'll spin out on the eddyline and have a hard time getting into the eddy. So if the differential is great or the eddy is extremely turbulent, you'll need some power to get through that powerful eddyline. A few strong, solid forward strokes generally do the trick; you don't need to sprint from 100 yards upstream.

WHERE TO AIM. Terminology identifying the parts of an eddy gives you a way to describe the area you're aiming for. The upstream end of the eddy is *high*; the downstream end is *low*. *Deep* refers to the area well within the eddy, and the borders of the eddyline are *close*.

Whether you're a beginner or a more advanced paddler, it's best to aim high in the eddy. This is where the eddy is usually smoothest and where the eddy-current differential is greatest. A turn here will be solid and crisp. But don't aim so high that you hit your bow on the downstream side of the rock (hitting a rock head-on is called pitoning). Since there is a tendency to err by hitting the eddy too low, try to hit the eddy high. Even if you fail, you'll still get in the eddy. If you aim low, however, and end up lower than expected, you may miss the eddy entirely.

When setting an entry point, keep in mind that the current is always fastest next to the eddyline, where the water has accelerated off the pillow (see Chapter Five). Compensate for this by setting your angle slightly more perpendicular to the eddyline. By the time you actually cross into the eddy, the faster eddyline current should have adjusted your angle.

CONTROLLING THE TURN. You're in the eddy. Now what? If you're a beginner, you'll want to do some form of the high brace, which will give you both support and a fulcrum around which to turn. Make sure you place this stroke inside the eddy; if you put it in too early, while still in the current, you probably won't get much of a turn. Maintain your inside lean until the boat slows down and you're off the eddyline. You can increase the sharpness of your turn by lifting your upper arm a little (turning the high brace into a partial bow draw) and pulling the bow toward the paddle.

As you gain experience, you'll want to control and adjust the sharpness of your turn by doing a full-fledged duffek or bow draw in the eddy. The duffek allows you to constantly regulate the arc of the turn. You may even want to come into the eddy with a closed duffek blade. Although this won't augment the turning due to the eddy, your blade will be ready to make corrections. If you want to make a wide turn or go deeper into the eddy, adjust your blade angle so that it's parallel or just slightly open, and don't do much of a draw. If, however, you want a sharper turn, open the blade more and put some power into the draw in order to execute your duffek quickly. A fast and powerful draw increases the speed and shortens the radius of

EDDY—TURN STRATEGY

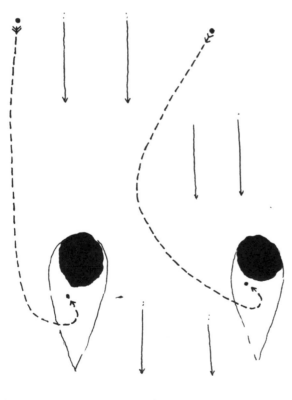

BAD APPROACH   GOOD APPROACH

Many paddlers, afraid of missing the eddy, come down right on top of it and attempt to set an entry angle at the very last moment. This causes the boat to slow at the critical moment of entry. Set the angle in advance and maintain boat speed across the eddyline, even if it causes you to travel a longer path. You'll be rewarded with an easy, crisp turn.

your turn. In general though, the better you get, the less you'll need to rely on an open blade angle.

TIPS FOR ADVANCED PADDLERS. The single most effective thing you can do to get an awesome eddy turn is to set a broad entry angle. It's a fine line between success and overkill, though, as too great an angle will spin you out before you've punched through the eddyline. The more perpendicular to the eddyline you are, the easier it is to turn the boat back upstream. Trial and error is the best teacher here. It's difficult to hit an eddy well and with enough speed from a spot directly upstream. Executing a last-minute sweep helps some, but then the boat will not have the speed to penetrate the eddyline. Do whatever it takes to improve your entry angle. If need be, get a good angle by paddling away from the eddy and then heading back. You travel greater distance, but the dramatic improvement in your eddy turn makes it worthwhile.

Additional speed helps get you past the eddyline. You'll get the best turn by carving a smooth, wide arc through the deep part of the eddy, even if this line is longer than staying close to the eddyline. This works because the wide turn allows you to maintain your boat momentum. To get deep into a turbulent eddy, you may have to sweep on your upstream side to keep from getting eddied-out on the violent eddyline. If the eddy is truly powerful, you may have to keep your sweep in the water and hold a stern draw in place (rather than a bow draw) to keep from eddying-out too fast even after you're past the main eddyline. Feather your stern draw directly into a bow draw for grace and efficiency.

SPEEDING UP YOUR TURN. If you want to quicken your eddy turn, lean forward at the waist as you cross the eddyline to throw some weight into the bow. This causes the eddy to grab more of your bow's hull and turn you faster. Another way to get a sharp and immediate turn is to insert the duffek fairly far forward, say 2 feet up from the hip but still a foot or so from the side of the boat. If you insert this duffek just into the eddy side of the eddyline, you can harness the power of the eddy as soon as possible. This position doesn't allow you much time or space to do a bow draw, but if you do the stroke quickly, you'll still get a fast turn. Try this move in conjunction with a forward lean to get an even quicker turn.

SIDESLIPPING. When carving an eddy turn, you may notice that the boat tends to sideslip somewhat. This happens when your boat plows sideways through the eddy rather than carving a distinct turn. Any boat will sideslip, but the extent depends on the boat's design. Boats with hard chine or rails—most slalom boats, for instance—sideslip less than boats with soft rails. You can minimize slipping with two techniques. One method that's good in soft-chined boats is to lean to the inside. The more you lean, the less it'll slip. If you have a boat with harder chines, you can minimize sideslipping by leaning the boat very slightly to the outside of the turn. The outside rail digs into the water, preventing the boat from skimming sideways on the surface. Yes, this goes against the maxim to always lean to the inside of your eddy turns, but rules are made to be broken. Leaning to the outside of the turn also makes your turn sharper. On the other hand, the boat's momentum also tends to die sooner, so be ready to take a forward stroke on either side to maintain the boat's speed. Don't lean too far to the outside because this will cause you to stall out or flip. Five degrees should be plenty.

STAYING IN THE EDDY. To stay high in an eddy or to keep yourself from falling out the downstream end, convert your duffek or bow draw into a forward stroke. By doing this, you can immediately pull yourself upstream without taking your blade out. Feather the duffek into position and pull on your forward stroke. Apply force to the paddle only when the boat is facing upstream or back toward the direction you came from.

Doing this stroke combination allows you to maintain your boat's speed, an important consideration if you want to exit the eddy immediately with a ferry or peel-out.

HITTING SMALL, NARROW EDDIES. You may want to try to ferry into narrow or small eddies (sometimes known as microeddies). These can be difficult; you need enough momentum to get into the eddy, but not so much that you blow through and enter the main current or collide with the riverbank. Adjust your speed accordingly.

As you cross the eddyline, do a small, snappy duffek and quickly convert it to a forward stroke. This tactic keeps you from flying straight through and out the opposite side. It also keeps you high in the eddy, an important consideration, since small eddies quickly peter out downstream.

Peel-outs

Getting out of eddies and heading downstream are just as important as getting into them. This move is called a peel-out. A good peel-out depends on that familiar trio: lean, angle, and speed. A peel-out is almost exactly like an eddy turn, but reversed. As with the ferry, you need to lift with your upstream knee to lean the boat downstream so that your upstream edge doesn't catch. Lean just before you exit, and level the boat out only after you have reached the same speed as the current. As with the ferry and eddy turn, the greater the eddy-current differential, the more speed you'll need to keep from getting spun out on the eddyline. Exit with an angle of 45 degrees or more to the eddyline. As with the ferry, the more angle you have, the more speed you'll need.

To do your first peel-outs, set your angle, get some speed, lean the boat, and place a high brace on the downstream side of the boat. The blade gives a pivot point, and as long as the boat is moving more slowly than the current, water will move under the blade, providing some support. Use feathering to convert your high brace into a forward stroke to accelerate yourself on downstream.

If you're more advanced, pull your high brace in toward the bow like a bow draw or duffek. This will help the current turn you while also giving you some bracelike support. Once you're turned downstream, you can then convert this quasi-brace–duffek into a forward stroke.

PEEL-OUTS FOR THE ADVANCED. The best way to peel out is with a downstream bow draw or static duffek. Your duffek can be placed out to the side and drawn in toward the bow, or placed up near the

PEEL-OUT ANGLE

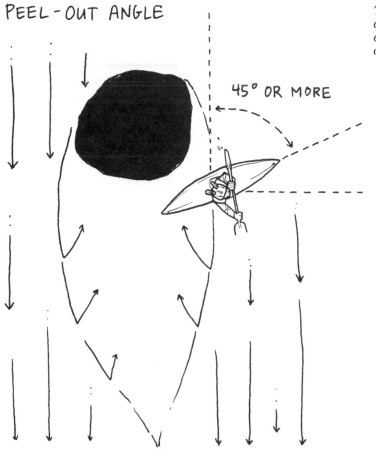

45° OR MORE

The peel-out requires a downstream boat lean and an exit angle of 45 degrees or more.

bow (the static duffek) and turned into a forward stroke when the boat becomes stabilized and has stopped turning. The duffek provides stabilization as well as control and correction—just as it does when you make an eddy turn.

You can do an immediate peel-out by inserting your downstream turning stroke in the current as soon as the current starts pushing the bow downstream. You can tighten the turn by taking a sweep stroke on the upstream side as you exit. Remember to keep the boat leaning downstream throughout. If you want a wide, arcing peel-out, ferry out from the eddyline a bit before placing your turning stroke in the water. Do this stroke only after the boat has already

The peel-out. Some exit speed in the eddy helps the boater cross the eddyline in control.

The boat is crossing the eddyline at a 40-degree angle. You can increase your stability and the turn's effectiveness if you present the hull to the current by doing a downstream lean.

started turning downstream; let the current do the initial work. If you ferry out too far, you'll lose the turning energy that the current differential imparts to the boat.

Once you have good balance and the correct amount of speed and angle, you can insert a combination stroke that is part forward stroke and part draw. This is the smoothest way to do a peel-out; the current

Half of the boat is in the current and half is in the eddy. The current is pushing the bow downstream while the eddy is holding the stern in place. The stroke is a support and turning stroke and the boat is leaning downstream.

The peel-out is complete. The boater is doing a stroke to help the boat achieve current speed, the speed at which boat stability is greatest.

does almost all the turning and you only need to help it out a little while you accelerate downstream.

Just as you ferried out on a wave, you can also peel out on one. As your bow turns downstream and the middle of your boat rides over a wave peak, apply power to your bow draw. If you time this right, you'll peel out, spin on a wave peak, and turn downstream with almost no effort.

Putting It Together: The Eddy Turn—Peel-out

As you become more competent at individual eddy turns and peel-outs, think about combining them. Unless you have a reason to scout or rest, why do an eddy turn, stop, and paddle again to gather up exit speed? Why waste gasoline by braking unnecessarily? Use the momentum from your eddy turn and channel it directly into your peel-out. As always, you can do a ferry instead of a peel-out.

To combine the eddy turn with a peel-out, do an eddy turn and point yourself upstream or even slightly toward the eddyline. Finish your duffek when your boat has traveled 180 degrees and is pointed directly at your peel-out exit; then you can just paddle straight

Putting the eddy turn and the peel-out together. A left sweep brings the boat into the eddy with the correct angle. If you have the right speed, you can enter the eddy almost perpendicularly.

An inside, or upstream, boat lean with a bow draw produces a fast, smooth turn.

The bow draw–duffek is put in toward the bow in order to tighten the turn. This will put the paddle in forward stroke position without taking it out of the water.

The boat crosses the eddy-line with a downstream lean. The forward stroke is nearly complete.

Heading out. A downstream stroke helps turn the boat and pick up speed.

ahead. It's most efficient to turn your duffek directly into a forward stroke, but depending on circumstances, you may need an additional stroke or two to get to the eddyline. The fewer strokes you use, the better. The important thing is to keep your boat moving; if it stops, you lose energy. Try to keep your duffek blade parallel to the boat; you'll slow down less.

SOME STRATEGIES FOR DIFFERENT BOAT DESIGNS. Whether you're eddying or peeling out, the design of your boat affects the quality of your turn. With an awareness of some handling differences, you can adjust your technique to maximize the performance of your boat. A longer boat, for instance, is usually faster than a shorter boat, and enables you to gain a lot of speed for your entry or exit. The more speed you have, the more angle you can set.

A shorter boat, being slower in a straight line, means you have to peel-out with a smaller angle than if you were paddling a longer boat. Extremely short boats, though fun for playing, can be a little tricky to eddy-turn well since they tend to spin out very easily on the eddyline. This is also true of boats with a lot of rocker. The best way to compensate for this is to get as much speed as you can and optimize your entry angle. With a boat that is fast in a straight line but turns poorly, start your turns early to give the boat time to get around.

You may have to lean more if you paddle a boat with hard chines. As mentioned previously, hard-chined boats allow you the option of using an outside lean. A soft-chined boat is relatively forgiving. Because of its rounded hull, it needs less lean when crossing eddylines, sideslipping aside.

S Turns

An S turn is, appropriately enough, an S-shaped maneuver used to traverse an eddy or current. S turns are sequential combinations of eddy turns and peel-outs. They come in two forms: eddy S turns and current S turns. Done either way, S turns allow you to move quickly through a rapid. You can replace a peel-out with a ferry at any time, making the basic maneuver even more versatile.

EDDY S TURNS. These can really zip you across an eddy. Because you maintain the boat's speed across the eddy, you have momentum going into the exit, whether it be a peel-out or ferry.

To do the eddy S turn, enter the eddy as you would with a typical eddy turn. Now, before the eddy has a chance to grab the bow and turn you upstream, convert your duffek into a sweep. Most eddies are strong enough that you'll have to do a powerful stern draw on your upstream side to keep your boat from completely eddying out. Do allow your boat to turn upstream slightly, at about the same angle you used to cross the eddyline, but with the bow pointed up relative to the eddyline rather than down. This will set your angle for

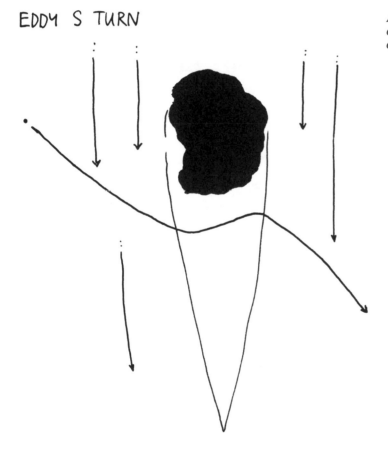

EDDY S TURN

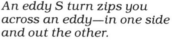

An eddy S turn zips you across an eddy—in one side and out the other.

The S turn. Current is flowing from top to bottom. A right sweep sets the angle between boat and eddyline. A good S turn requires the boater to have a fair amount of crosscurrent speed. Notice that the paddler is aiming high in the eddy where the eddy is strongest.

A duffek is placed in the eddy to turn the boat ever so slightly upstream. The boat is leaning upstream into the turn.

a standard peel-out. If you want to ferry out the other side of the eddy, set a ferry angle before you exit. When setting your angle, take your speed and the current differential into account. If the eddy's about a boat length wide, you can traverse it with a single Duffek–sweep combination. To get across a big eddy, you may have to take a few forward strokes after you finish your duffek–sweep. As you paddle across the eddy, smoothly adjust your line along the way to achieve the correct exit angle.

Remember to lean the boat upstream as you enter the eddy and downstream as you exit. You can really get whipped across a small powerful eddy, so be ready to lean downstream on your way out.

Without being taken out of the water, the duffek has quickly been converted into a stern draw, which keeps the boat from turning upstream into the hole. The boat is still high in the eddy and tilted upstream.

The exit. The upstream lean has been replaced with a downstream one.

CURRENT S TURNS. These are almost the same as the eddy S turns, only done from eddy to eddy. The current between the eddies is what turns you. When you peel out into the current, don't turn completely downstream—you'll want to have some crosscurrent velocity to get into the eddy on the other side of the chute. After you peel out, set the appropriate angle for entering the second eddy.

Lean downstream as you exit the first eddy and upstream when you enter the second.

FERRYING OR SURFING INTO AN EDDY. Another version of the eddy-to-eddy maneuver across the current is the ferry. You won't do an S turn per se, but you will effectively jet across the current without los-

A current S turn has the same S shape but it's done from eddy to eddy, across a jet of current.

CURRENT S TURN

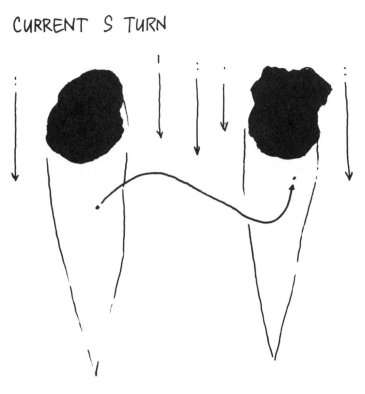

ing ground. The faster the chute, the farther upstream you need to point. The hardest part of this move is breaking through the second eddy, especially if the eddyline is powerful; you're pointed upstream and it's difficult to cross an eddyline well with this entry angle. You can compensate in two ways: increase the speed of your ferry to give yourself warp speed, or turn your boat perpendicular to the current just before hitting the eddyline. To do this, put in a powerful forward sweep on your upstream side. Sweeping while the center of your boat is on a wave peak, even a small one, makes this maneuver easier.

At times, you'll be entering an eddy while ferrying on a surf-wave. The same technique applies, but you need to be even quicker with your strokes because the wave makes you travel faster. With the correct combination of angle and speed, you can get an extremely snappy eddy turn.

SEVEN

Play Paddling

PLAY PADDLING—the art of wave surfing, endering, and hole riding—is an extremely rewarding way to plug into a river's flow. The learning process is an incredible journey into the subtleties of a river's personality and power. Along the way you'll experience frustration, disappointment, and maybe even fear; above all you'll have lots of great times and some magical moments when it feels like you, your boat, and the river are in total harmony.

Getting Ready

Playing is one of the best ways to improve your kayaking skills and your confidence on the river. By practicing in nonthreatening play spots, you can try things you would never dream of doing on a regular river run. You will get better, fast. You can then combine these moves with all your other river-running skills to become a more complete paddler.

Each play spot you find will have unique subtleties and peculiarities; all are little puzzles waiting to be solved. Try to understand what the water is telling you and what patterns of movement it will allow. Experiment and analyze; change your approach, timing, and emphasis to find the solution to each spot. Work smoothly and fluidly with the water. Get outside your-self to watch what you are doing, and watch others. Learn to use your body creatively, working all the quadrants of the boat. And finally, don't take the whole thing too seriously (it is play after all). The river is the great equalizer.

After a brief discussion of some essentials (equipment, the roll, and conditioning), it's on to the nuts and bolts of play paddling.

EQUIPMENT. Good play boats are generally short (12 feet or less) and have soft chines plus a fair amount of rocker for easy spinning. A low-volume kayak, with a flat tail and hard rails, will be a responsive wave-surfing vehicle but will be harder to control in holes. Plastic boats are great because you can play with abandon without worrying about breaking your boat. In play holes, plastic boats are also much easier on you than glass ones; plastic is flexible and absorbs some shock that would otherwise be transmitted to your body. A good fit in the boat is crucial for maximum control (see Chapter One).

Any paddle will suffice for playing, but ones with dihedral blades work particularly well. They are forgiving and tend to climb up to the surface when you are bracing or rolling. They also have an efficient back-blade shape for low bracing and backstrokes. Small to medium-sized blades are best because they are easier to move around in the water.

Dress warmly. When playing, you're going to get really wet. If you're cold, you won't enjoy it very much. Throw the insulation layers on and top these off with a good paddle jacket, drytop, or drysuit. On still colder days, add a beanie for your head and neoprene gloves or pogies for your hands.

ROLLING. The roll is the cornerstone of all play paddling. Without a good roll you won't have the confidence to try things that might lead to a flip—and in play paddling, that includes almost everything fun. In fact, when playing, you should figure that if you're not going upside down now and again, then you're probably not learning as fast as you could be. Some hours spent in a pool grooving your roll until it's instinctive on both sides will pay big dividends on the river. You should also work to learn a hands roll. Even if you never play on the river without a paddle, just knowing you can roll with only your hands will be a big confidence boost.

Conversely, river play is a great way to perfect your bracing and rolling skills. Practice definitely makes perfect. You'll learn to roll quickly and creatively in white water by feeling and using the water. Rolling in the river usually isn't any more difficult than in a pool, it's just different. You should concentrate on keeping your head down as you come up, and if rolling on one side doesn't work, quickly switch and try the other side. If you believe you will come up, you will.

CONDITIONING. Play paddling can be hard on your body. You'll be more tired after a couple of good hours in a play spot than you would be after a normal river run. Play spots also isolate stress on specific parts of the body (like the elbows, when you are playing in holes). To minimize body damage, keep a few things in mind. The larger muscle groups located in your lower torso and stomach are much stronger than your arms. Think of this torso area as your balance and power center and use these muscles as much as you can when playing. The shoulder is a wonderful joint with a huge range of motion, but it's particularly vulnerable to injury if its range of motion is maxed out. Avoid injuring it by keeping your elbows down and in and leaving a little flex in your arms for shock absorption. Also, always rotate your torso toward your strokes.

Off-season conditioning, especially of the shoulders and torso, makes great sense. Not only will you be less susceptible to injury, but you'll also be able to paddle for greater lengths of time. Most injuries occur after long layoffs or in the early part of the year when the water is very cold and you're not in shape. Stretch well before you start paddling and make sure to warm up before taking on any maneuvers that torque your body. Finally, when your muscles and tendons start screaming at you to stop, listen to them.

Wave Surfing

Surfing is a good starting point for all play paddling. The skills learned here form the core of more complex play maneuvers. The goal in surfing is to get your boat onto the upstream face of a wave and stay there, gliding endlessly downhill on a rushing, pulsing roller coaster of water. Two main forces are at work: gravity sliding the boat down the wave, and the friction from the current pulling it back up. A third set of forces is the combination of rudders, paddle strokes, and body moves that you supply to orient the boat on the wave face.

GETTING ESTABLISHED. Your first task is to get onto the wave. The easiest approach is to ferry out with some momentum from an eddy beside the wave. Ideally, your boat speed and the downstream current speed cancel each other out and you can easily slide across onto the wave face. Start by picking a small, well-formed wave at the base of a drop that has a nice run-out for easy rolling and also a big eddy on at least one side that you can use to get back up to the wave. Usually, there's a small diagonal depression feeding off the eddyline into the trough of the wave. Look for this and try to visualize your boat ferrying across it, with the boat tilted slightly away from the oncoming current and your body leaning back to keep the nose from being buried. Often, if the diagonal is well defined and

Wave surfing—gliding endlessly downhill on a rushing, pulsing roller coaster of water.

regular, it's your free ride onto the main face of the surf wave and you can glide out effortlessly.

If the current is fast or the diagonal irregular, start low in the eddy and get a few good strokes to gather speed before you hit the eddyline. Punch out with a very shallow angle to keep from getting spun down stream. With enough speed, you may be able to cruise across using a rudder or stern draw to keep the boat aligned and ferrying toward the wave. If you find yourself on the back face of the desired wave, try to paddle onto the next downstream wave in sequence or quickly abort your attempt and get back in the eddy for another shot. On your next attempt, adjust with more or less speed, a better ferry angle, or a higher approach. Once you get the hang of coordinating your speed and angle, you'll be able to cruise right to the spot you want.

On some waves upstream of the eddy or in very swift current, you have to power all the way onto the wave and don't have the luxury of using a rudder stroke to stay aligned. In these situations, use sweep strokes to keep your boat straight. Don't use a rudder because it doesn't provide any active forward propulsion. If you do, the boat speed will slow and you'll blow downstream past the wave.

You can also catch waves by paddling hard forward as you drift backward from upstream of the wave. This method is difficult, as well as inefficient, because getting lined up is tough when you can't see where you're going, and often you won't be able to stroke hard enough to negate the current. There are some wonderful waves out, however, that have no close eddy, and this may be your only chance to catch them. Instead of backing onto the steepest part of the wave, aim for the edge where it's flatter. From there you can see and control your entry onto the steeper face.

STAYING THERE—SURFING. As you slip across onto the wave, lean back a little to slow down, place a rudder behind your hip on the side you want to turn toward, and then push the paddle blade out to turn the boat perpendicular to the wave face. If the boat is sideways to the current, this rudder becomes an upstream brace, which could flip you, particularly if you also lean the boat upstream. At first, try to stay fairly straight on the wave. When you rudder, keep the boat flat from side to side, or even tilt the upstream edge up a little so that water can't pile up on the boat's edge. Concentrate on using your knees to control the edges.

The rudder–sweep combination is your main wave-surfing stroke. Behind your hip, vertical, and next to the boat, the blade acts like the skeg of a surfboard and keeps the boat straight. Sweeping out pushes the back of the boat around, or if the blade is already away from the boat, pulling it in moves the tail toward the blade. Play with variations of this, including slightly changing the blade angle in the water, to control your boat on the wave.

Moving your body back and forth helps you stay on waves. If the bow is pearling, or burying, lean back to slow the boat and pull the bow up. Combine this with a hip tilt to get the bow to climb up to the surface. You can also move your paddle blade out to the side, perpendicular to the boat, and drag about half the blade to slow the boat and help pull the bow out. If you're slipping downstream off the wave peak, lean forward to get some weight going down the face and throw in some fast, short paddle strokes. Press your feet down into the trough as you paddle; pulling up hard with your knees pulls the boat back out of the

Front surfing. Use a combination of rudders, paddle strokes, and body moves to adjust your boat angle and stay on the wave. Here, the current is flowing right to left and the paddler is using a rudder–sweep combination to keep the boat tracking straight.

wave. Sometimes stabbing a rudder between your windmilling forward strokes is effective in turning the boat. Try to anticipate and not to overcompensate; in time you'll learn to subtly shift your weight.

By now you're probably carving little zig-zags on the wave face. As you try to keep the bow up, you'll discover that an angled kayak fits better on most waves than one pointed straight upstream. The steeper a wave is, the more you have to angle your boat to keep the nose from pearling, so your turns need to be quicker and sharper. Since you have to expose a lot of your boat edge to the current, make sure you lift with the knee on the paddle side to keep the upstream edge high, and lean back slightly. As the boat starts turning, shift your boat lean the other way (lift your other knee), into the turn toward your rudder. This makes the boat carve in a tight turn. If your boat has a flat tail with sharp edges, it will carve better on its outside rail. This means you'll lift the edge next to the rudder throughout the turn. But with most medium- to high-volume boats, initiate the turn to the outside and then lean into the turn as the boat arcs around.

These are the surfing basics. There's a whole wide world of waves out there waiting to be glided on, massaged, ripped, and shredded.

Back Surfing

After you get front surfing wired, it's time to reverse the controls and try back surfing. You have to be more attuned to your boat and to the wave because you can't see much of what's going on behind you. You quickly find out how much you've been relying on your vision, rather than your sense of motion. You'll need to spend lots of time going backward until your body can instinctively sense where the boat is on a wave.

Maintaining speed and ferry angle to get onto the wave face is tough; in fact, it's often harder than staying on the wave. One solution is to backpaddle onto the wave from upstream, but it's difficult to slow down enough to catch the wave and you only get one shot at it. If you can ferry out to the wave face from a side eddy, you'll have more success. With a wave that abuts an eddy, you can go all the way to the top of the eddy, ease onto the eddyline with little speed, and after the current whips you around (watch your upstream edge), use a powerful reverse sweep to push yourself onto the wave.

BACK SURFING TECHNIQUE. When you back surf, the pivot point of the boat moves toward the bow and your knees become the most important control points. Lift with the knee next to your reverse sweep turning stroke to initiate a turn and then crank up hard with the other knee as the boat comes around. Normal body position is slightly forward in order to keep the tail up. If the stern starts to pearl, lean farther forward and tilt the boat slightly. If you're washing downstream off the top, lean back, throw in some quick backstrokes, and work to push your butt down into the trough. This will get your center of gravity off the crest of the wave. Once you're back onto the wave face, you can continue your slashing.

Get your paddle into the thick of the action. To turn, use a front rudder. Place the blade near your feet, about 4 inches to the side, with the power face out and back blade edge angled slightly in toward the boat. Keep your top hand near shoulder level and move it in or out to control the blade in the water. If you need to slow down without turning much, lower your top hand, move the paddle out perpendicular to the boat and drag about half the blade in the water. Sweep strokes will also work to turn the boat if you're high on the wave peak where the boat spins best.

Backsurfing takes a lot of practice but once you start to get the feel of it, you'll be amazed at what you can do. In fact, it's possible to rip as effectively going backward as forward.

ADVANCED FRONT AND BACK SURFING. Big, fast waves aren't necessarily more difficult to surf than their smaller cousins, but getting onto them is. After your first ride on a big screamer—your boat hums and skips and the spray peels your eyelids back—you'll be hooked for life. It takes an aggressive mind-set to catch these waves; you really have to want to be out there to make it. As you scout out the situation from a convenient eddy, concentrate on a perfect approach and look for any diagonal feeder waves that will help funnel your boat across to the main wave

Back surfing. You have to rely on a feeling for where the boat is on the wave because there are few visual cues. Body position is slightly forward to keep the stern up. For a front rudder, the paddle is inserted with the power face out and the back edge angled slightly toward the boat.

face. Get a good head of steam up before you leave the eddy, and power out. Any reverse strokes here and you're history; you'll slow down and be swept past the wave. Use sweep and power strokes to keep the boat aligned. Once you get on the wave, go wild. Big waves have large wave faces, so take advantage of them. You may be able to sit there in a holding position, but for a great ride, try ripping from side to side, dropping into the trough, turning quickly and then zooming up and whacking off the top.

Really steep waves pose even more of a problem. Two strategies work well here. One is to hang your boat at the very top of the wave and not let it go down into the trough. Balance and boat position are tenuous; too far back and you slip off the top, too far forward and you crash down into the trough. Quick reactions are essential; use subtle weight shifts, rudders, paddle brakes, and quick forward strokes to stay balanced and moving back and forth on top.

The other strategy is to get the boat sideways as it crosses the steepest part of the wave and then bank and turn off the corners where the wave edges are less steep. Timing is everything. Trying to surf steep waves can be frustrating if you keep pearling or blowing off, but there is no better way to build up your wave-surfing reflexes. When you finally do find the groove, it will all be worth it.

Two specific paddle techniques will really help

your back-surfing turns. Sliding an angled front rudder right into the boat by your foot will provide pressure on the bow and help push it around. This is exclusively a plastic boat technique if you cherish your paddle. Or, set your normal front rudder and pull the blade toward you with your lower hand while initiating the turn. This requires strength and an aggressive style, but if you can do it, it really speeds up and tightens your turn. The boat will snap around 90 degrees or more on each rudder. Don't forget: with back surfing, it's mainly your knees doing the work.

The next step is hands surfing. First, make sure you have a hands roll. Swimming out of a flip is definitely bad form. The basics for hands surfing are the same as for surfing with a paddle except that you have relatively little power. Compensate with more exact weight shifts and a finer feel for the wave. To get a taste of hands surfing, hold the paddle in one hand and use your other hand as a rudder, and then switch to turn the other way. Once you jettison your paddle, make up for your lack of power by taking long, powerful strokes with your hands. To turn, rudder on one side and sweep forward on the other simultaneously. If you need to slow down, simply drop both hands in and catch as much water as you can to create resistance.

Surfing two (or more) boaters on a single wave is a blast. Now that there's another projectile out there, you really have to be in control. Peripheral vision, communication, and anticipation are crucial. Figure that you have your piece of the wave and they have theirs; stay in your own area. Be careful, particularly with the top blade of your paddle, when stroking right next your partner. Crisscrossing is a great move, but it takes a fairly large wave face. Time the crosses so that one person is climbing up and across as the other is dropping way down and under. It's the responsibility of the top person to bail off the wave peak if a crash is imminent. When you're back surfing with another boater, it's nice to be on the bottom for the cross because you can grab the other boat and pull yourself under if you're not quite going to complete the cross.

In surfing, you're limited only by your imagination. For new challenges, try these:

• Surfing with your eyes closed.

• Front surfing lying on the back deck and watching the wave behind to stay lined up.
  • Weaving crisscrosses with three on a wave.
  • Paddle twirling.
It all leads to better boat control, greater confidence, and more intimate look at the river.

Enders

The ender, or endo, is a classic play move. The mechanics are simple. Drive the end of the boat down and bury it deeply in the trough of a wave or hole. This temporarily stores buoyant energy under the surface. As this energy is released, it pushes the boat up vertically; the more energy you can tap into, the higher you fly. Depending on the hydraulic and how your body is aligned, there are a number of ender variations ranging from 45-degree-angle "pop-ups" to full air shots, where the boat is thrown vertically out of the water.

A myriad of hydraulics can provide enders. The most obvious ones are medium or large waves and most holes. Less obvious is the diagonal hole that forms at the head of some eddylines when water pours steeply around a rock. In a good ender hydraulic, the water decisively forces the boat end down and is also deep enough that the boat doesn't get clobbered. Watch where better paddlers are popping enders to find the good spots.

Boat volume and design affect your enders. Low-volume boats are easier to get vertical but don't give nearly the air time on an ender that a high-volume kayak does. Body weight is also a factor. Boats with small, round cross sections in the ends are better for doing spinning ender moves and are somewhat easier to get lined up because there's less edge to grab and throw you off.

Enders are notoriously hard on boats. There's a lot of force at work as the boat dives deep and current loads on the deck. If a rock stops the process, something has to give. In a glass boat, it might be the entire boat end, and the forces can easily crinkle the deck of a plastic boat. Probe gently at first if you like your boat, or stick to enders out of nice deep wave trains.

ENDER TECHNIQUE. The key to a good ender, aside from having the right hydraulic, is your line-up.

All your wave-surfing skills come into play here. Ferry and surf your way across to the steepest part of the hydraulic and then rudder to make sure you are lined up to drop straight down. Never rush the line-up. Try to set up high on the hydraulic so that you're essentially falling off the top into the trough. Work to stay in alignment, and as you feel the water catch and pull the boat down, let your body go with the flow and follow the boat in. If the boat veers as you drop into the trough, you'll auger in to the side and probably flip. You can sometimes prevent this from happening by holding yourself in vertical alignment with a low brace. Either an ender happens or it doesn't—you'll certainly know it when it does.

Experiment with your entry angle. Often, especially with a diagonal hole off the edge of a boulder, if the boat drives down straight upstream, the bow catches too much water and gets pushed to the bottom and crinkled. Leave the rocks on the river bottom in peace. In these situations you'll get better enders by setting up with the boat at an angle to the current rather than directly into it.

You're heading up. What now? With your weight forward, the current will sweep the bow under you, and as the boat comes up, it will somersault—a guaranteed ender, but also a guaranteed face blaster. For maximum air, lean onto the back deck and stand on the foot pegs when the boat fires up. Pushing up with a low brace also sometimes adds height. In either case, if you want to spend less time under water, set up to roll while you're still in the air. It's tempting to reach for the water with your paddle as you crash down, but this can really wrench your shoulders. It's safer to remain compact and keep your arms in close to your body.

To avoid flipping, spin 180 degrees or pirouette out of the ender after the boat has reached vertical. You can rotate to the side of the boat with your head and shoulders, or use the paddle to help get the spin going. One way is to reach across the deck and plant a vertical paddle cross-bow (see Chapter Eight); the position looks like a roll setup. Untwist your body as the boat starts to come up. The cross-bow works great to start a pirouette, but when it fails, it usually results in a face-plant because the setup is a very unstable position. Another way to get the boat spinning is planting the paddle to the side of the boat and using a sweeping backstroke on the horizontal plane.

For back enders, use your back-surfing skills to get lined up and then let fly. Your body weight is low, and there is a strong tendency to pull your knees toward you, so back enders are usually the end-over-end, somersaulting, nose-filling variety. You can avoid this by pressing skyward and a little downstream with your feet and leaning back. This keeps the boat balanced vertically instead of falling over on top of you. Catching the water with a duffek results in a quarter or half twist and an easy roll the rest of the way. With or without a paddle, back pirouettes are difficult; a draw sometimes works to initiate rotation.

ADVANCED ENDERS ARTISTRY. It's possible to conjure up one, two, or even three full revolutions while on end. For multiple pirouetting enders, the best hydraulics are where water is pouring steeply around the side of a rock. You drop the nose in near the rock and then tap into the current rushing by the side to supercharge the revolutions. Start the rotation going in the current direction by reaching cross-bow with your paddle, doing a horizontal sweep stroke, or if you have no paddle, stretching across and planting both hands in the current. The closer your body is to the axis of the boat, the faster the rotation will be. This is the same principle that a spinning ice skater exhibits; as the skater's arms are drawn in, the spin accelerates. Your body should be up and back, tight against the boat, with your head and torso leading in the direction of the spin. If you sit up perpendicular to the boat, you will kill the rotation (the natural tendency is to spin once around and then sit up). For maximum spins, stay tight to the boat and just keep milking the revs, even when the boat starts back down.

Enders give you a chance to lose all your inhibitions and behave like a foolish kid. Anything goes:

• Spin your paddle as you ender, pass it behind the boat, throw it away and then hand roll.

ENDER WITH PIROUETTE

To avoid flipping, pirouette out of an ender after the boat has reached a vertical position. A pirouette can be initiated with a rotation of head and shoulders to the side, a sweeping backstroke on the horizontal plane, or as shown here, by planting the paddle cross-bow.

• Slow your ender down, balance vertically, and then pogo along downstream.

• Link your enders front into back.

Ender sessions are often limited only by how much water your sinuses can take.

Hole Riding

Playing in holes is a little more intimidating than wave surfing. To be good for playing, the hole must have a size and shape that can hold a boat sideways. You may initially view holes as a threat, but with improvements in your technique and a greater understanding of holes, you'll discover how much fun they can be. And in the process, you'll become much more at ease on the river.

In order to get the most out of playing in a hole, you have to know what the water's doing. At first glance a hole seems to be a frenzied pit of negative ions and possibly negative experiences. Closer inspection will reveal the current patterns. The current accelerates as it flows over an obstacle. As it meets slower water, it piles up. Some falls back down, forming the white, aerated, upstream face, and the rest flows off the back downstream. Finally, the water is flowing by the sides, sometimes hooking toward the hole's middle at the corners. You'll have to tap into these currents to make things happen.

Holes come in numerous sizes and shapes (review Chapter Five for a complete discussion). In general, stay away from holes that have water flowing in steeply from upstream, or which are ledgy. If the rock that is forming the hole is close to the surface, stay away. If you flip upstream in these, you may bang into the rock. Also avoid deep holes that you'll have to climb way up at the corners to escape, and holes whose ends angle severely upstream or butt up against a rock. If a corner angles downstream (a smiling hole), it will be easy to get out of, but it's unlikely to be a great play spot. Initially, be conservative about which holes you go into. Start with benign surface holes that have gently sloping bottoms. You can then work into the bigger, trashier spots after you have a solid base of experience. Watch the hot paddlers; they gravitate to the good spots.

SIDE SURFING. When hole riding, unlike when wave surfing, you normally sit sideways parallel to the pile. The easiest and least stressful method for entering a hole is the same as for catching a surf wave. Ferry across from an eddy on the side, but when you get to the shoulder of the hole, instead of ruddering straight, let the water take your boat and ease it into a parallel park position. If you slam hard into the hole and plant a high brace, you'll usually blow right through downstream, and possibly tweak your shoulder as well.

Make sure to keep the upstream edge of your boat tilted up. If you don't, the water flowing in from upstream will load up on the boat's edge and force it under, flipping you upstream. The steeper the water pouring down from upstream, the more radical this boat lean needs to be. If it's a gentle hole with a wide bottom, it won't take much lean. Try to lift the edge with just your knee, and leave the rest of your body fairly upright and balanced over the boat; this is the key to all good hole playing. Relax and feel the boat float, but don't let it rock from side to side. The natural tendency is to plant a high brace and lean your body into the pile for support; fight this urge and rely on balance instead. You can put in a medium-high brace if you absolutely have to, but keep your elbows bent and both hands below chin level, and don't stretch downstream. Experiment with flattening the boat to see how little boat lean you actually need.

Side surfing. The key to all hole playing is to balance your body over the boat. The upstream edge of the boat is tilted up with the knee so that water flowing in from upstream (the right) can't catch the edge, but the body remains upright and centered. The paddle is low to take advantage of strong torso muscles.

If you do get flipped upstream, tuck forward tightly and keep your paddle close to the boat so that you don't bang the rock or get the paddle ripped out of your hands. Then, roll on the downstream side (it's the only side that will work). This roll is normally ridiculously easy because the current is pushing your body under and bringing it back up on the pile. Often, just slowly sliding the paddle into a brace position will bring you upright. If you do a full roll setup, go easy with your sweep and make sure to keep your upstream edge high as you come up or you'll get "window-shaded".

After you're comfortable hanging out, it's time to start moving around. Use powerful, low sweep strokes in the pile. Keep the paddle well below shoulder level to take advantage of your strong torso muscles. This is where balance really comes into play; if you lean your body into the pile and you have a high brace planted, it is extremely hard to get any lateral movement going. Once you get used to moving around on low paddle strokes, you won't want to just sit in a hole on a static brace. Backing up is very efficient because you can get your body over the paddle and really use your torso muscles to push your way back. If you want to exit, just paddle out a corner. Once you start climbing up the corner, don't relax; paddle until you're completely out.

Practice sitting and moving in holes on both sides. On a river you don't always get to choose which way you face.

ESCAPE (OR "WHAT TO DO WHEN YOU'RE REALLY GETTING WORKED"). Someday, when you're paying more attention to the beautiful surroundings than to the river, you may find yourself snapped up and rudely chewed by a sticky hole and be unable to get out. Then, you'll think back and wish you had read this section.

If you really seem stuck, first try to relax your mind so that you can think rationally about what you're doing. Most holes have one corner that is easier to get out of, so find it. If you can't climb out that corner, try moving back to the middle or even the opposite end of the hole, and then get a run across and try to carry some boat speed into the escape corner. Some of the worst holes to get out of are deep and short because it's hard to get up a head of steam.

If the run at the corner doesn't work, climb as high as you can and then flip to the outside, away from the hole, where current is going by the side of the hole. This current will usually catch enough of your body to pull your boat out. If you flip toward the bottom of the hole, you'll probably be rolled under the boat and pop right back up in the exact spot where you started, but disoriented and with a nose full of water.

There are a number of other theories about how to escape a sticky hole. A common one is for you to flip in the hole's middle and then reach down with your paddle to catch water flowing underneath. This opens up your body to rude treatment and possible injury. Another idea is to reach over the top of the pile and pull out with a high brace. This is dangerous to your shoulders and it will work in only the very smallest holes. A third common theory is to ender out. In a truly sticky side surf, however, it's very difficult to get turned perpendicular enough to ender. And even if you can get turned, enders in a bad hole often lead to an uncontrolled cartwheel scenario. The best method is to aggressively work to the corners to escape, flipping to the outside if necessary. Of course, anything counts, as long as it gets you out with ego and shoulders intact.

Working to get out of a bad hole can be exhausting. If you've given it your best shot and are still stuck, punch out of your boat while you still have some energy left for the swim. If there's a crowd watching, it's probably best to look casual before you swim. But with common sense, practice, and a bit of luck, you may go through your whole paddling career without ever getting truly stuck. Hole-riding technique goes hand in hand with escape technique.

SPINS. Spins, the next logical step, are the bread-and-butter maneuver of hole riding. A spin is a 180- or 360-degree rotation of the boat as it sits high on the pile of the hole. As you work to unlock the puzzle of spins, you'll find another world out there, but it takes a lot of hard play and some flips to find it. To spin, you have to bring a number of things together: balance,

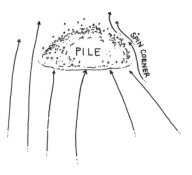

PLAY HOLE WITH SPIN CORNER

A nicely shaped hole for spins. Here the main portion of the river is to the right and most current is pushing in from that side. As a kayak climbs up at the lower right corner, the current feeding across the top will push the end of the boat toward the middle and help the spin.

boat sense, edge control, timing, paddle dexterity, and commitment.

The ends of the kayak must be relatively free to spin, with no water pressure on them. You have to position your boat at the right place on the hydraulic—high on the pile and usually near a corner. There are some wonderful exceptions; you can sometimes catch a surge in the middle of a bouncy hole and go for a spin. Normally, however, you'll be working a hole's corners. Certain hole shapes can really help. A jet of water at the corner feeding back across the top of the pile toward the middle will help the boat spin. If the hole has no corner return, or if the corner angles downstream, you might not be able to spin at all.

You'll have to adjust your approach to the spin spot depending on the hole shape. In some holes you

360-degree spin sequence. The paddler is using momentum and a powerful forward-sweep stroke to climb up the pile at the hole's corner. Speed control is important—too fast and he will blow off the corner, not fast enough and he won't get the boat up high to spin it. Body position is balanced and upright.

The boat is now high on the pile and both ends are free and can rotate. The paddler has flattened the boat and is spinning it with a sweep stroke. His body is leaned a little forward to free up the stern. The hole's corner return is also helping the spin by pushing the bow toward the center of the pile.

can just float the boat high on the pile until you feel less pressure holding the ends. With others you'll have to paddle hard to the corner and pull up with a strong sweep stroke, or carve down and then up fairly steeply to get the ends loose. Develop a sensitivity to what the water is doing to the boat. If it feels like the ends are caught under the backwash, find a new approach or a different spot on the pile. Try to control your speed going to the spin spot; too fast you'll blow off the top, not fast enough and you won't be able to get high enough on the pile to spin.

Concentrate on keeping a relaxed, balanced, and upright body position. As the boat climbs up, flatten it from side to side and turn it with your paddle. As you drop back into the trough, change to a new upstream edge. Strive for a quick, fluid transition—edge up, flat-

As the boat drops back in, the paddler switches to a new upstream edge. He will continue to carry momentum backward and carve down and then back up to climb to the spin corner.

The process is repeated, only this time it's a front spin. Do a quick, fluid transition: edge up, flatten and turn, and switch to a new upstream edge going back in. After the spin rhythm is established, it's time to start working in other maneuvers.

ten and turn, and switch to a new edge going back in. If you don't commit to the whole spin, you'll get hung up on top with the boat spinning one way and your body refusing to go with it. This is the ubiquitous 179-degree spin and usually leads to a quick flip or an ender. In fact, many enders (particularly back enders) are just failed spin attempts.

To turn the boat, use a nice low sweep stroke. You might also try a bow draw to pull the front of the boat around in a back spin, or a rudder to pry the back around in a front spin. In a perfect spin spot you won't need a paddle at all; a balanced body position and fluid edge transitions will be enough.

Often a little upper-body prerotation helps spin the boat. Start the rotation going with your torso and the boat will be forced to follow. Forward and backward weight shifts are also important. You want to keep your body as upright as possible, but sometimes you may want to lean your body up out of the hole to help free up the end still in the bottom.

ADVANCED HOLE PLAYING. Advanced hole riding is the culmination of the art play paddling. Fluidly link a series of dynamic moves, and join with the water in a high-energy, graceful ballet. Find the rhythm that is appropriate for each hole. Work to smoothly link your spins and experiment with varying their rhythm. Notice where they tend to stall and where it is easy to break out of them and drop into the hole to initiate other moves. Mix it up, try different sequences, and work as many different maneuvers as you can into the dance.

Hands hole playing adds another dimension to your play. It's a great way to further refine your boat and body control. And it's fun. Some moves, like spins, are almost as easy with hands as with a paddle, since you can brace on both sides at once, your balance is good, and you have no paddle to slow you down. Power is limited, so be more aware of what the water will allow you to do. For spins, you usually have to get a run at the corner to reach the spin spot. To turn on top, simply forward sweep with one hand and reverse sweep with the other at the same time. Intentional windowshades are incredibly easy; flip upstream (tucked tightly), go with the flow, and sweep your hands out on the pile side to bring yourself up.

A few other things to try:

• Hold your paddle in one hand and then change hands as you spin. (Throw in paddle twirls here for flash.)

• Do a pirouetting ender without blowing out of the hole (a Polish ender). Slow the ender down, hang your upper body far forward into the hole, and finish it off with a quick body rotation to the side. This is usually followed by a quick roll on the pile, and then you're ready for another.

• Drop in backward at a slight angle and tilting the boat a little upstream. Plant a duffek downstream to keep you from falling over; your boat will rocket up and around the planted paddle (a wingover).

The sky is the limit with hole playing and new tricks are continually being discovered. A new move usually evolves when something good happens by accident. Then you have to figure out how to do it intentionally. Be open to new patterns.

Whitewater Rodeos

The first whitewater rodeo was held in 1976, on the Salmon River. Since then the popularity of rodeos has mushroomed. Currently, about ten rodeos are held annually, and they occur throughout the paddling season (late April through early August). Many rodeos include a slalom and downriver races and a squirt boat event. The main focus, however, is the freestyle, or hot-dog, event. Most events have women's and men's classes for all skill levels. Rodeos are great places to see old friends and meet new ones, check out the new play-paddling moves, and strut skills in competition.

River and eddy etiquette become even more important in rodeo situations, especially in the mad crush before the event begins. A lot of keyed-up people are on the water, flying out of ender spots, blowing off waves, and bouncing around in the eddies waiting their turn at the play spot. Be especially courteous and aware of the other paddlers. Don't monopolize the play spot during practice; once you've done a maneuver, move on and try something else. Some bumping in the eddies is inevitable, but try to minimize it. Watch out for paddlers making their final approach to the play spot; slight crowding or a small bump here can ruin timing and concentration. The idea is for everyone to enjoy the water; don't get so wound up that you forget this.

STRATEGY. Listen carefully when the judging criteria are explained and then plan your rides for maximum points. Try to choreograph the entire ride in you mind, and then go out and execute it. You probably won't get the ride you want, and then you'll have to do some improvising, but always start with a solid game plan.

There's a lot of background noise, and to do well, you must block it out and concentrate on the ride. Try to relax and focus on paddling to your full potential. It's as much a mental ride as a physical one. Believe in your ability.

The Ultimate Goal

Take the word of a certified play paddler, Doug Ammons:

"Finally, when you intuitively feel the proper balance combinations, the leans, the rudders, the timing of aggressive strength and gentle touch—these coalesce into your personality. There comes a time on the water when you feel as though you know where every bubble is, sense every current, instinctively time each surge, and smoothly absorb its power. And at last you will be set free, gliding gently and serenely in the midst of apparent chaos, with the sunlight sparkling in the spray all around. This is the alchemy of play-paddling—becoming enveloped in the music and magic of flowing water."

EIGHT

The Next Step

YOU NOW KNOW MANY OF THE BASIC WHITEWATER maneuvers: ferrying, eddy turns, peel-outs, and surfing. The river is nearly yours. The trick now is to combine these basic maneuvers with each other and with the other more advanced maneuvers presented in this chapter. Your goal is to use your skills effectively and with confidence in the midst of a rapid.

Running Rapids

Angle and speed are your two primary tools for tapping the river's resources. When you master these, time spent on the river becomes easier and more rewarding. Fighting the river is always a losing proposition, so relax and let the river do most of the work.

Take advantage of all a rapid has to offer. Floating down a relatively easy rapid can be done in an innertube with almost as much finesse as in a canoe or kayak. But really using the water well is an experience superior to just surviving a rapid. Knowing a smattering of a foreign language can get you around, but just getting around doesn't compare with the world that fluency opens up.

Get into the habit of looking for all the holes, eddies, waves, and river anomalies, even on easy white water. Practice your surfing, ferrying, and eddy turns even when the water level is only modest. There's always room for improvement; high-water snobbery will only rob you of the opportunity to improve.

Running harder and harder rivers each time you go out is not the only path to paddling excellence. Although "hair boating" is great for thrills, chills, and spills, you may end up terrified if your skills aren't up to snuff. Practice, experiment, try play paddling, or paddling up rapids. You can challenge yourself as much as you want without risking life and limb.

EFFICIENCY. Maintaining your boat's momentum is essential to performance paddling. The best way to achieve efficiency is minimizing correctional strokes. Know what you want to do and where you want to go. Read the water and be aware of its effects on your boat. This will allow you to use more positive strokes (strokes that drive or steer you) and fewer negative strokes (such as correctional rudder strokes and reverse sweeps). Maintaining boat speed saves you energy; you don't have to reaccelerate the boat every time you do a stroke or maneuver. The more you eliminate unneeded strokes, the more energy you'll have for maneuvers that require serious exertion. Keeping your speed up doesn't mean that you have to sprint and hammer away every minute you're on the river. It just means that combining moves will save you from having to build up another head of steam between them.

TIMING. The river has its own rhythm. If you can tune into this and become one with the river, you'll be immersed in the pleasure that river kayaking is all about. Even if your whitewater technique is excellent, there are so many variables on the river that you'll always be improvising to some extent. If you can improvise well, you can stay in tune. Knowing what to do and when to do it is the constant challenge of whitewater kayaking. Good timing takes practice, and time in the boat is the only way to get it. There are times to be passive and let the water take you, and there are times when you need to be aggressive and make things happen. Find a balance. If you're doing an eddy turn into a peel-out, for example, it's often better to let the eddy's energy turn you while you steer. Then, when your peel-out angle is correct, you can pull hard on a few strokes to exit the eddy.

MORE RIVER JUDGMENT. Paddle conservatively until you know and trust your capabilities. Be attuned to your feelings; they'll tell you whether you should run a rapid or not. There seem to be two distinct kinds of fear. The first is invigorating: you're apprehensive, but you also feel a sense of anticipation and excitement at coming face to face with a challenge. You know you can meet the challenge and gain strength from the experience. The second kind of fear is debilitating: instead of planning your route, you're wondering whether they'll be able to find your body.

As long as your abilities are roughly matched to the challenge, it's probably good to push yourself when feeling the first kind of fear. The fear-excitement feeling provides you with energy and helps you focus on the task at hand. To make progress in any endeavor, you must push yourself at times; the trick is to make each step forward small and manageable.

If you're petrified by fear, however, why push yourself? Portage, if that's what's best. Whitewater kayaking can be scary enough without running rivers before you're ready. Don't allow yourself to be coerced into running something if you don't feel reasonably confident. The fear saps your strength and blurs your vision, and river running in this state is neither safe nor fun.

RIVER ETIQUETTE. There are a few basic courtesies that help make river trips safer and more enjoyable. Don't pressure other boaters into paddling something that's beyond their skill or comfort level. Give others a fair chance at a play spot; wave hogging is greedy.

There are also aquatic versions of traffic lights. On the river, the right-of-way is always granted to the paddler coming from upstream. If you're surfing a wave and someone is coming toward you, it's your responsibility to move out of the way. Right-of-way should always be given to less experienced paddlers, since it's easier for a better boater to move around. When eddying out above a drop, the first boaters in should make room for subsequent paddlers. This is especially important in microeddies above blind drops. If possible, less experienced boaters should be closer to shore. This will allow the more experienced paddlers to exit first and run the next rapid.

RESPONSIBILITIES OF THE FIRST ONE DOWN. The first one through a rapid, usually the group's best paddler, should wait at the bottom to assist others if necessary. Assistance can be from the boat, or from shore with a thrown rope. Also, the first boater down should point with a paddle to where the cleanest route is. Always point in the direction others *should* go, never to a trouble spot. You don't want to direct someone right into a nasty place. If you decide a rapid is too risky once you've run it, lay your paddle horizontally on top of your head to signal others to stop. Then you can motion for others to either scout or portage.

Using Eddies and Holes

Eddies are invaluable for getting down the river with style. Eddy-hopping down a rapid breaks it up into small, manageable sections. The perfect eddy is distinct from the rest of the current, but many eddies are caused either by rocks below the surface or by a shallow area of the river. These eddies may not be readily apparent, but with practice you can learn to see them. Some of these eddies have small boils. Others appear flatter than the rest of the current; waves in this slack area will be smaller. They look like slow-moving water rather than proper eddies.

Learning to spot these eddies is critical to fine-tuning your river running. They will turn your boat and force you off-track if you hit them unexpectedly. They can be used to your advantage, however, if seen in advance.

You can use any kind of eddy to turn your boat if you're sideways in the current. Just as putting your bow in an eddy will spin you backward on the eddy-line, putting your stern in one will turn you downstream. If you find yourself backward, you can put your stern in an eddy to spin you back downstream.

USING A HOLE TO TURN

By placing the bow or stern in a hole or an eddy, you can use current differentials to spin the boat effortlessly.

Holes can be used in many of the same ways as eddies. You can use them to turn a little or a lot, depending on how much of your bow or stern you place in the hole. It's often easier to turn your boat 270 degrees using an eddy or hole than it is to turn 90 degrees without one. You can also do S turns and eddy turns across the backwash. In addition, you can perform these same moves just downstream of the backwash, since the presence of a hole often creates a usable, though sometimes turbulent, eddy immediately downstream.

Side surfing a hole's backwash from end to end is another method of traveling cross-current. You can even stop and scout from a hole. As long as you can get out of them easily, they offer relatively stable vantage points. Be sure you can get from the hole to shore if you don't want to run the drop.

Rebounding off Pillows, Diagonal Holes, and Waves

Any formation that provides upstream force can be tapped to yield crosscurrent momentum. The basic idea is to turn yourself into a well-controlled human pinball and ricochet off stoppers and pillows. Downriver racers often use this technique to minimize the amount of turning and twisting they have to do. This allows them to stay in the most direct line. The more diagonal the wave, hole, or pillow, the more you'll get flung laterally and out the downstream end. Big pillows are particularly adept at bouncing you off to the side if your boat is upstream and—this is critical— already on that side. As always, lean into the hole, pillow, or wave. As you come into contact with the pillow or backwash, stab a brace into the froth. The angle of your deflection will depend primarily on your speed and angle of contact, as well as on the direction and force of the water.

Adjust your deflection angle by positioning your brace so that the blade is somewhat vertical. That way

You can shoot yourself to one side of a rock if you hit the pillow at an angle and with some speed. Always lean the boat into the pillow while your brace is in.

PILLOW RIDING

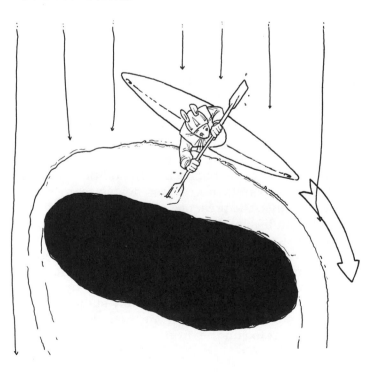

you can do a combination sweep stroke–high brace. Keep your high brace low to increase stability and provide you with some turning and forward momentum. You can vary the speed and direction of your exit by adjusting the amount of sweep you do.

Extremely powerful, wide pillows can actually have eddies just upstream of the rock. These provide a big buffer between the current and the rock. If these pillow-eddies are big enough and conditions are safe, you can eddy out above the rock. Although this is a fun and wild spot to hang out, only experienced paddlers should try this move. Get some experience first by playing on angled pillows or the corners of more regular ones.

Rock Gardens

There are several techniques you can use to maneuver through rock-filled sections of river. The tried and true back ferry is a good option (see Chapter Six). S-turn maneuvers are extremely handy for dodging behind and around rocks. You can also use draw strokes to pull yourself sideways to one side of the rock without using a slowing backstroke. Combine this draw with a deflection off a pillow to bounce to one side of the rock. Drawing yourself sideways is especially useful if you are getting too close to a steep bank or headwall. In these situations, a sweep stroke would knock your stern against the wall, which in turn would lever your bow back toward the wall. The draw, however, pulls the whole boat sideways, allowing escape. Remember to lean slightly away from your draw. This will permit an easier draw, and it will prepare you for a lean into the obstacle should contact occur.

Waterfalls and Steep Drops

Before you run a steep drop, you'll want to ask yourself the following questions:

• Can you make it to the spot where it's best to run it?

• Can you recognize that spot from upstream, in the boat?

• How high is the drop?

• Are there rooster tails or other hazardous protrusions sticking out of the face of the drop that could snag you?

• How's the hole at the bottom?

Ski jumping takes you over the hole at the bottom of a drop. The more speed you have, the better. Pick your landing spot carefully and be wary of subsurface obstacles.

SKI JUMPING

• Are there rocks or obstacles at the bottom that you could bow pin or piton on?

• How's the washout for paddling or swimming?

Assuming the answers to these questions indicate a runnable drop, the best way is to ski jump it. If done correctly, ski jumping should keep you from plunging straight down into the bottom hole. You have to know exactly where to aim and then paddle hard for that spot. The more speed you have, the better, so try to get as much of a running start from upstream as you can. As you approach the lip, or edge, of the drop, you'll want to lean back a little to help keep your bow from diving down, and take a final power stroke at the drop's lip. Flex your abdominal muscles and lift with your knees to keep your bow up as you take this last stroke.

The goal of ski jumping is to land the boat fairly flat in the pool at the bottom with some downstream speed. Ski jumping helps you miss the worst of the hole at the drop's bottom. The more air you get off the lip, the better you'll be able to avoid the hole at the bottom. It's easier to get air with a really steep drop; a slanted drop can take you right into the hole. Landing is called *pancaking* or *boofing*. If you land correctly (and the drop isn't too high) the landing can be quite smooth. If it's a high drop, landing flat with no speed is a good way to compress your vertebrae. Keep your speed up. As a rule, waterfalls more than 10 feet should be considered high-altitude and treated with an additional dose of respect. Whatever you do, *never* run a waterfall sideways. There's no better way to get yourself stuck in a bad hole.

Some spots are choicer than others for running a waterfall. It's best to run the drop where the bottom hole is least sticky and where there are no obstacles. A perfect waterfall often has its fastest water in the middle, just like a consistently straight riverbed. So the middle can be a good place to run the drop if the hole at the bottom is safe. It depends on the drop, however, since the middle can be either where the hole is the worst, or where a good chute exists.

If the hole is nastier at the middle, you may want to consider running the drop diagonally. If you want to end up on the left side of a drop, it's often best to start on the right. In fact, this rule of thumb applies to run-

WATERFALL RUNNING

If you can find a clear path and if the hole below the drop is runnable, route B is best. If the hole is nasty in the middle, running the drop from side to side (route A) is an option. This route requires you to have lots of diagonal momentum.

ning many rapids, especially those which make a sharp turn. To run one side of a drop, start from the opposite side in order to gain the necessary angle and momentum. Make sure to get up a lot of speed, above the drop. Set your angle as far in advance as possible. This will minimize the need for last minute, and possibly unsuccessful, corrections. If you aim correctly, you'll land to the side of the hole's maw—in a kinder, gentler part of the hole, in slower moving water, or in an eddy.

Whatever the case, you'll need to be ready to do an eddy turn or to brace on the downstream side of your diagonal approach if you land in slack water. If you're spot-on, you can use the technique described in the next section to avoid bracing. However you land, keep your paddle shaft well away from your face.

Paddling Downstream Through an Eddy

This isn't a meat-and-potatoes move like the eddy turn or ferry, but it's a handy technique to have in your repertoire. It can be used to keep yourself from being eddied out when you come over a drop, small or large, into an eddy. It's basically an extreme S turn where your goal is to hit the eddy and exit on the side you entered rather than going out the opposite side. It's a great test of timing and stroke skills.

If you can get a direct approach from upstream, the eddy will be less able to spin your boat upstream. Conversely, the greater your angle to the eddyline, the harder it will be to avoid being violently eddied out against your will. When doing normal eddy turns, a big angle with the eddyline maximizes your turn. But with this technique, you want to minimize the effect of the eddy. The eddy has a lot of energy pushing you in one direction. The trick is to redirect that energy so that it moves you in the direction from which you came. The stern draw is just the tool you need to accomplish this.

Get up a fair head of steam and hit the eddy, leaning back a little to prevent the bow from being grabbed instantly by the eddy. *Just* as the eddy starts turning the boat, do a powerful stern draw on your upstream side to counteract the eddy's power. Lean your boat to the same side as your stern draw in order to speed your turn and help with the transfer of energy. The

A down in an eddy. Current is flowing from right to left and the boat is completely within the eddy. Note the powerful stern draw and the boat lean, which keeps the eddy from grabbing the boat and turning it upstream.

stern draw has to be extremely powerful and held in place for as long as possible. The force from your stroke should overcome the force of the eddy. The real skill is knowing when to insert the stern draw; if you insert it too soon, you finish your stroke while the eddy still has some power and you get eddied out. And if you wait too long before doing the stern draw, the eddy takes control of so much of your boat that even a perfect and extremely powerful stern draw can't pull you out of the eddy turn. Either way, you get punished with an undesired eddy turn. Try to do it without inserting any back strokes. Despite their effectiveness, they stall the boat.

After the eddy's power has more or less dissipated, but while you still have some speed, switch from your stern draw to a duffek on the other side. Transfer to this stroke quickly or the boat's speed will die while the paddle's out of the water.

Paddling Upstream

The ability to get back upstream can be extremely handy if you've cornered yourself and don't want to continue down the river without scouting or portaging. In addition, paddling upstream provides an excellent opportunity to practice your whitewater technique. It requires polished water-reading skills and efficient use and placement of all strokes, since all your strokes must drive your forward; a reverse stroke will push you back downstream. It also makes for great strength training. If you can paddle up a particu-

PADDLING UPSTREAM AROUND A ROCK

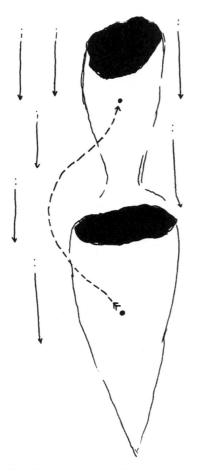

It takes some speed to paddle upstream around a rock. Lean back as you exit the first eddy to prevent your bow from burying. Cut back as soon as possible to let the eddy's current move you upstream.

lar drop, you can paddle down it three times as well. It seems as though paddling upstream is directly opposed to the axiom, "let the water do the work." And it is, if you're just grunting away upstream in midcurrent. But there are numerous tricks to minimize your energy output and let the water help you. You end up using the same techniques that spawning salmon use to make their way upstream. Fish, and paddlers, rely on eddies to make their leaps over ledges, to rest, and to initiate their ferries.

The best strategy for paddling upstream is to look for eddies and areas of slack water that you can get to sequentially, from the first eddy to the next, and so on. Look for areas of slack or slow-moving water and connect them, even if your route looks somewhat schizophrenic. You may have to ferry back and forth to find the eddies, waves, and routes that will get you upstream. Surfing, ferries, and S turns, are all useful maneuvers.

EDDIES. Eddies are invaluable for gaining upstream yardage. You can eddy-hop upstream just as you can downstream. Use eddies for resting and regaining the energy you need to continue your upstream trip. If you position yourself on an eddy's downstream end (without falling off the downstream side), you'll have the maximum runway length for building up speed. An efficient forward stroke and quick acceleration will give you more speed when you hit the current.

If two or more eddies are placed in line with each other on the same side of the river, two strategies help you gain altitude. Which technique you choose depends on the size of the rock, the speed of the current, the length of the eddy, and whether enough water's coming over the rock.

If the water coming over the rock is deep enough (it need be only a few inches deep—just enough to slide your boat over) and not too fast, not too steep and not too high (less than 1 to 1½ feet) and if you have enough speed, you can paddle right up over the rock. If the rock is above water, however, you have to ferry out in the current and, as you paddle upstream, ferry back to the same side. Use only forward or sweep strokes. Often the current is too fast for you to get away with doing any kind of reverse stroke. If you can get to the second eddy on one or, at most, a few strokes, lean to your downstream side as you exit the first eddy and paddle hard upstream. If done properly, the downstream offside lean helps you turn into the upstream eddy without having to execute many slowing correctional strokes. If it takes more than a few paddle strokes, flatten your boat and hammer away with powerful and efficient forward strokes.

Your destination may be crosscurrent or upstream or both. When this is the case, you need to power out of an eddy and ferry over and up to the next eddy. If the second eddy is narrow, ferry with your bow more upstream than usual to keep from flying straight through the opposite side of the eddy.

You can also use regular eddy turn–peel-out combinations to accelerate yourself upstream. This is called an eddy-turn slingshot. Enter the eddy from the side, rather than from upstream. Speed from your eddy turn augments your brief sprint up the eddy. Consequently, you'll have more boat speed than if you just paddled from a standstill at the downstream end of the eddy. There's a trade-off in this move that's worth consideration: if you hit the eddy high, you get into the strongest part of the eddy, but your runway distance decreases. All in all, the eddy-turn slingshot is an especially good move if the eddy isn't very long. An advantage to this technique is that this eddy exit angle may give you a nearly optimal angle for your upstream paddle. You can get the most from the eddy by hitting it low to give yourself space to accelerate. Get up as much speed as possible before exiting.

An S turn is a great maneuver for picking up some momentum when you want to traverse upstream diagonally. If you hit an S-turn eddy, you can fly up the eddy by augmenting the eddy's upstream current with your own strokes. This S-turn slingshot effect is similar to the eddy-turn slingshot—you're just exiting the other side. When you come out of the eddy, you'll have additional speed to get over and up to your destination. This is an effective tactic even if you have room to execute only one or two strokes: a perfect example of letting the water work for you

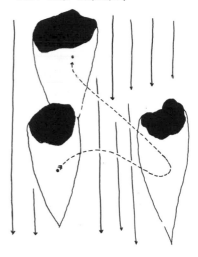

EDDY-TURN SLINGSHOT

You can put the slingshot effect to use to accelerate yourself upstream. This move is a good choice if paddling upstream around the rock isn't possible.

The S-turn slingshot is also an effective move for preserving boat momentum.

S-TURN SLINGSHOT

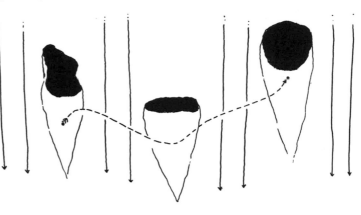

Surfing a diagonal hole or wave is a great way to combine surfing skills with upstream paddling techniques.

SURFING A HOLE UPSTREAM

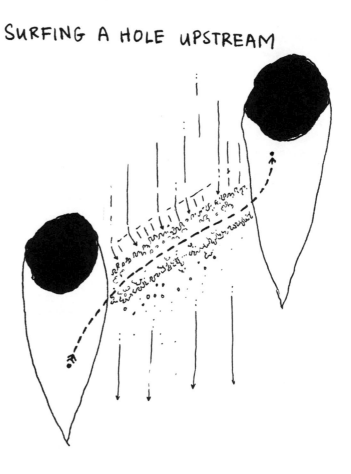

SURFING. If there's a diagonal wave or hole with its upstream end in either an eddy or slack water, you can often surf it and simultaneously travel upstream. You can also side surf a diagonal hole upstream. Depending on the size of the wave, you may have to paddle while you surf, but you'll probably only be able to take safe and effective propulsion strokes on your downstream side. This upstream traverse is an especially hot move if the wave is perfect for surfing, but it can still be quite effective if the wave is a tiny little thing. It's convenient when the wave begins and ends on two eddylines, but rare. Many times, you'll have to power upstream or do a hard ferry to get to a surfable wave.

ROCK POLING. You can also move yourself upstream by poling off rocks. It may look more like rock climbing than paddling, but there are times when it's extremely effective. The timing is somewhat tricky, since you want some upstream speed as you pole off a rock. Place your poling stroke just as you travel upstream past a solid obstacle to get the best boost. You can pole without having previous speed, but it's not nearly so effective. Switch quickly between poling and paddling. You don't want to lose the momentum you just gained. Be careful not to catch your blade between rocks; you could snag or break it.

Playing Games

Inventing games on the river is a great way to have fun and improve your skills without necessarily taking the risks inherent in hair boating. There are lots of ways to challenge yourself with river games. For example, paddling upstream can be a river version of mountain climbing; do it purely for the fun and challenge. You'll learn helpful new river strategies and tactics. You may even be surprised by the steepness of the rapid that you can overcome.

MAKING MOVES. One fun game to play is making up a river puzzle with a sequence of whitewater moves, and working on it over and over until you've mastered it. It's best to pick a sequence that you can "recycle on" by paddling either up an eddy or up a small drop to regain your starting point. Recycling allows you to try the same sequence over and over.

For example, peel out of an eddy into a fast chute, S turn behind a boulder, surf a wave into another eddy that you trick by paddling down through it without getting eddied out. You can make any combination of moves, from easy ones to extremely difficult ones. Try to do the whole sequence as smoothly as you can, or as quickly, or with as few strokes as possible. Or try all of the above at once. In any case, maneuver through the sequence using as few correctional strokes as possible. Strive for consistency; making a move or sequence once might be luck, but nailing a maneuver time after time is undeniable evidence of proficiency.

TAKING NEW LINES. Paddling the same old route on a local run time and again may lead to boredom. The thrill of excitement and discovery evaporates. Most paddlers get into the rut of running not only the same line time after time, but also the easiest path, because that's the route they did when they first ran the river. On most rivers, there are usually some less apparent and more difficult routes in other areas of the same rapid. If you experiment with your standby runs, chances are you'll find some new action.

ONE-BLADED PADDLING. Try paddling using only one blade. This is a good game to play on flat water, on the river, or in slalom gates. It will improve your boat control, because maneuvering your boat with only one blade is tricky. You have to get used to cross-bow maneuvering, which is an awkward exercise at first. It's like being a beginner all over again. The boat turns when you don't want it to and doesn't when you do want it to. But as your one-bladed skills advance, you'll be able to see the improvement even when you go back to using your "training" blade.

Practicing one-bladed, cross-bow technique will teach you to control your boat through subtle leans. You will also become more sensitive to minute shifts in the boat's momentum. This sensitivity will help your timing—that intuitive sense of when to do what stroke. And finally, who knows? If you should break a paddle halfway down a run sometime, you'll have the skills to go on.

When doing cross-bow strokes, always maintain your control hand position, even though you may be tempted to change it to ease your forearm twist. Doing a forward cross-bow stroke is difficult because it's hard to get the power face pointed directly backward. Keep trying, though; you'll get it with practice. Cross-bow sweep strokes are especially difficult because it's hard to get your paddle very far from the boat. You have to lower and cross your arms considerably to get a good arc. The cross-bow sweep is terribly inefficient as well as awkward; your sweep arm is crossed in front of your chest and is upside down from a normal sweep position. But since it's all you have to work with, it's best to be stoic.

The cross-bow duffek is, in some ways, more effective than a regular on-side duffek. The cross-bow position allows you to get the paddle completely vertical; you gain a lot of physical leverage from this position, unlike the cross-bow sweep. The cross-bow duffek is especially fun, albeit challenging, when you're doing eddy turn–peel-out combinations. You really have to have correct angle, speed, lean, balance, and timing to maneuver well. You'll see great improvement in your overall performance if you can perfect this move.

Practice catching eddies, surfing, and maneuvering through rapids with one blade. By doing this, you

The cross-bow duffek. The boat is turning to the boater's left. The paddle is vertical and the blade angle is slightly open. This stroke feels awkward at first, but with practice it can be stable and very effective.

can make a Class II run seem as challenging as a Class III or IV. Combine your one-bladed technique with invented whitewater practice sequences to really improve your skills.

Pivot Turns and Stern Squirts

Pivots, or squirts, are maneuvers for putting one end of your boat underwater so that the opposite end comes vertically out of the water. Squirtists use subsurface current differentials to do all sorts of wild stunts and tricks. With a squirt boat, you can really turn the river into your own playground by doing maneuvers that high-volume paddlers can only drool over.

Given the size of the topic, there's not enough room to cover all the ways to squirt. See James Snyder's *The Squirt Book* for comprehensive and entertaining information on just about every aspect of squirt technique.

Basically, the squirt works because you impart a diving angle to either the bow or the stern of your boat. To achieve the dive, stern squirts require a low-volume stern with sharp edges that cut through the water. Because of this prerequisite, the only boats that can do stern squirts are squirt boats, slalom race boats, and a few low-volume plastic boats. Of these three models, squirt boats are the only ones low enough in the bow to do bow squirts consistently. Whatever type of boat is used, paddlers usually learn the stern squirt first because it's the easiest.

The force required to dive the boat's stern comes from a reverse sweep. In white water this reverse sweep, in combination with a subtle upstream lean when exiting an eddy into the current, causes the stern to dive quickly and deeply. You can continue the boat's dive almost indefinitely using a reverse sweep–bow draw combination, which is a feathering maneuver, or a reverse sweep to a forward sweep on the opposite side.

Practice pivots technique first on flat water to remove the least predictable variable—moving water.

FLATWATER SQUIRTS. When practicing the squirt on flat water, gather some speed and do a small sweep to turn the boat slightly in the direction the boat will pivot. This preturn is as important to the stern squirt as it is to the duffek stroke. Now, while the boat is gliding and turning slightly, lean the boat slightly—no more than 10 degrees—to the outside of your turn (see Chapter Three) and do a powerful reverse sweep on your inside (the concave side of your preturn). Keep your body upright or lean it to the same side you do your reverse sweep on. Dip your outside edge lower in the water than your inside edge. Arc the blade wide to get the most from your stroke; you'll have to keep your arms low. As you sweep, lean back ever so slightly to help sink the stern. The lower the volume of your boat, the less you'll have to lean back. You'll find, as you get proficient, that you don't need to lean back at all—the trick is in timing your lean with your reverse stroke. If you keep the boat leaned to the outside, the stern sinks and the bow goes up in the air.

When your reverse sweep nears the two or ten o'clock position relative to the bow, switch your sweep into a bow draw if you want to do reverse sweep after reverse sweep. This is done by flipping the blade 180 degrees and lifting the nonsweep arm to forehead level. The reverse sweep is now a bow draw. This transition between the sweep and the draw is tricky. Try to apply power evenly throughout the pivot—otherwise the boat stalls and the stern kicks up to the surface. This happens especially when the diving angle is too much and there isn't enough cutting stern speed. If you use a larger boat lean, you need a more powerful sweep to keep the boat from stalling and bobbing up.

As the draw approaches the boat's bow, slide the blade parallel with the boat from bow to stern while lowering your upper arm to assume, once again, the proper reverse sweep position. Do this transition quickly to keep the boat from stalling.

Since the stern is already underwater, every additional reverse sweep–draw stroke will bury the stern a little more. How deep your stern goes is inversely proportional to your boat's volume. You can do this stroke combination indefinitely . . . or until dizzines overcomes you. In lieu of a draw, you can take your blade out and insert a forward sweep on the opposite side. This maneuver is a little tricky because the stern tends to rise without applied paddle force; if the stern stops slicing through the water, it'll fly up to the surface. If you do a reverse sweep to a forward sweep on the other side, be careful not to lean forward as you plant your forward sweep—a natural reaction. Any forward lean with your body also brings your bow down and your stern up.

As you're pivoting, maintain an even and slight off-side lean. If your lean is too great, the stern dives too fast and stalls. An underwater stall causes the stern to pop up to the surface like a bubble—low-volume, but still plenty buoyant. On the other hand, if you don't have enough lean, the stern won't cut beneath the surface at all. A lean of about 5 degrees is all it takes.

SQUIRTING ON AN EDDYLINE. With a low-volume boat, an upstream lean, and the correct stroke timing, you can really get rocketed doing a reverse sweep stroke on an eddyline. The stern squirt goes against all your previous training because it requires you to lean the boat upstream as you peel out. Paddlers tend to be tentative about trying their first pivot turns in current because this normally gets them wet.

To do the whitewater pivot turn, paddle up the eddy and set your exit angle as though you were going to do a ferry. As the bow hits the eddyline, lean your boat slightly upstream and do a wide and powerful (but not necessarily fast) reverse sweep on your downstream side. As you lean your boat upstream, tilt your body downstream; although initially awkward, this will keep you relatively stable. Lean back minimally to put some weight over the stern. (As you get better, you won't need to lean back). You want to time your pivot so that the stern is underwater as it hits the current. If your boat is approximately perpendicular to the current as the stern crosses the eddyline, the energy imparted to your stern dive will give you the highest, most efficient pivot. Once the bow comes up, maintain your lean. Remember, if you change the lean abruptly, either the boat will stall out and then kick to the surface or you'll impart a climbing angle to the stern. Either way, your stern comes up and your bow goes down. If you effectively change your reverse sweep into

The stern squirt. A powerful reverse sweep, initiated close to the back of the boat on the downstream side, is done while the boater is still well within the eddy. The stern is already cutting slightly under the surface. Note the angle of the boat to the eddyline. Although the boat is angled somewhat upstream, the boater is leaning his body slightly downstream.

A moment later. The current is pushing the bow downstream and the stern is underwater and still in the eddy. The submerged stern is just about to come into contact with the current. The upstream boat lean and downstream body lean are especially evident.

Lift-off. As soon as the submerged stern hits the current, it's pushed down and the bow shoots up.

a draw and keep your bow up, you can pivot on down the eddyline, getting your bow higher and higher as you increase the stern dive. Keep your body over the eddyline as your stern cuts back and forth underwater between eddy and current. Try to time your strokes so that the reverse sweep is executed as the stern goes from eddy to current; this helps the bow gain altitude. Eventually, your boat may get so vertical that you do a rear ender with a flip. Fun!

COMMON PIVOTING PROBLEMS. There are several mistakes made by people learning the stern squirt. The most common is ferrying out too far before initiating the reverse sweep, which results in a weak, short-lived pivot. This is caused either by doing the reverse sweep too late or by exiting the eddy with too much speed. Amazingly, you don't need a lot of speed as you leave the eddy; a little is enough. With great pivot technique, you can pivot in the current instead of on the eddyline, but it takes more effort than if you let the current differential do it for you. Start your pivot before your stern leaves the eddy.

Trying to muscle the stern down as fast as possible is another common mistake. The trick to the pivot is timing and stroke placement, not 20-inch biceps. Again, speed isn't much of an issue; there's a point of diminishing returns. You have to pivot at a natural rate, a rate governed primarily by the speed the hull travels through the water. The stern dives through the water at a speed dictated mostly by the shape of the boat and the strength of the current differential, not your strength.

Keep your boat lean slight, as well as constant. If you do change the angle, do it smoothly. Also, remember to do a smooth, wide, arcing reverse sweep. If you do a reverse stroke instead of a sweep, the boat will drive backward, but the stern won't sink and spin.

OTHER WAYS TO STERN SQUIRT. There are other ways to squirt using eddy-current differentials. In fact, any safe place where a current differential exists is a good place to pivot. The biggest things to watch out for when squirting are pin spots and undercuts. Undercuts can be difficult to see. If you have any doubts, do your squirting elsewhere.

USING WHIRLPOOLS. For extra fun and altitude, you can augment your pivot by initiating it in a whirlpool. In turbulent water, a fair-sized whirlpool can really shoot your bow skyward. The whirlpool exerts a powerful force on the boat. Also, your boat tends to "fall" down into the whirlpool's eye.

THE CURRENT-TO-EDDY SQUIRT. Instead of squirting from eddy to current, you can go from current to eddy and get a great pivot. Paddle from the current toward an eddy with your bow pointed upstream at a ferry angle. Just before you cross the eddy-line, start a reverse sweep on your upstream side and lean the boat slightly downstream or toward the eddy. Normally, when eddying out you would lean into the turn, but in this case lean away from the turn. Knife your stern under the eddy; you'll get a squirt equal in power to an eddy-to-current squirt.

This type of pivot is smoother and easier to do if you initiate it on a "boil line," an area where a consistent boil comes in contact with the main current. Boil lines are usually found where water rebounds off a steep riverbank or headwall. A squirt works well here because boiling water shoots up above the surface in the middle of the boil, but it "falls" down under the surface at its periphery. This falling water helps submerge your stern.

PILLOW SQUIRTS. You can pivot on the line between a pillow and the current. A strong differential exists here; within a very small distance, fast current water becomes nearly still pillow water. This "pillow squirt" is a powerful technique, but don't attempt it unless you're competent. You can get pinned if you blow the move.

Paddling Different Types of White Water

White water takes on a different feel depending on its volume, speed, and riverbed. Big water, like that in the Grand Canyon, requires different paddling techniques and strategies than a small, technical creek does. Overall river competence includes versatility, the ability to adjust and adapt your style to the type of white water you're running. There is a wide spectrum of "types" of white water. On one end of the continuum the water is small, tight, and technical; on the other end it's big and powerful. You can also find big water that is extremely technical. This is the most challenging of all.

TECHNICAL WATER. A technical whitewater run is usually characterized by small, steep drops. Extremely steep runs are often called creek runs because these riverbeds are often dry except in flood. Be especially wary of strainers when running creeks. A lot of precision is required for a technical run because it has many obstacles, and pinning is a distinct possibility. In technical water, there's not a lot of leeway for being off-line. Be careful not to be sideways when negotiating tight, rock-strewn sections; you don't want to broach your boat between two rocks.

When the water is low, but the gradient steep, keep your bow up to run drops. Streams with little water often do not have deep pools after drops and you want to avoid bow pinning on subsurface rocks at the bottom of a drop.

In extremely tight rivers, you may want to paddle a short boat, one that's less than 12 feet long. This shorter length allows you to spin the boat quickly and easily when you need to. It also offers less boat surface for rocks to grab.

BIG WATER. In a riverbed that normally holds an average of 1000 cubic feet per second (cfs), any water level above 5000 cfs will start to feel big to most paddlers. At 10,000 and above, it will feel big to most everyone.

Big water is characterized by huge crashing waves, powerfully boiling water, and thrashy, inconsistent eddylines full of whirlpools and boils. The eddies that haven't been washed out are usually violent with powerful upstream currents and surging boils. The current is extremely fast and often unpredictable.

Because of the water's power, you have to be aggressive at some times and passive at others. There's no way to outpower the river. The lower you can keep your arms and paddle when executing strokes, the lower your center of gravity will be, thus providing additional stability in crashing waves and huge boils. Your propulsion strokes should have some brace component to them for additional support. There will be times when you have to lean your whole body into a crashing wave to keep it from flipping you upstream. The key is timing: lunge your body and put a brace stroke into the wave so that its force is met with yours. With luck, yours will win out.

GIVING YOURSELF LEEWAY. When reading big water from shore or the boat, remember that the water is moving extremely fast—probably much faster than it looks. Realize that because of this, things happen to you more quickly than on smaller, easier water. And, since the water is so turbulent, it will be difficult to keep your intended course without getting turned sideways or backward unintentionally. Figure the screw-up factor into your route-planning equation and have a good alternative strategy.

NINE

Slalom Racing

FLYING DOWN A WHITEWATER SLALOM COURSE is incredibly exciting; you're on the knife edge of disaster but in precarious control. You're fast and precise. When it's over you're exhausted, but also exhilarated from the thrill. This feeling is shared by both beginning racers and world slalom champions. After all, subjective experience is relative.

It's easy to recognize the best river runners: they have precision, grace, strength, and calmness. Slalom kayaking develops these strategic and physical skills. In addition, it heightens your ability to focus on the task at hand while staying aware of peripheral happenings; you learn to zero in on minute details and still keep the big picture in mind. These skills can be learned by doing a lot of river paddling, but slalom kayaking will quickly strengthen them. Slalom is a quantitative, almost scientific, approach to improving whitewater skills; you're given reference points (slalom gates) against which you can gauge whether you're efficient or sloppy, fast or slow. You get immediate feedback when you do a move well or poorly. Slalom success is measured by your ability to run the course correctly as well as by your speed.

There are many ways to run a course, but only one path is fastest. Thus slalom tests your analytical abilities as well as your technical skills, both of which are important elements of river running. Slalom skills can be cultivated on flat or slow-moving water, allowing you to practice without driving some distance to the nearest whitewater run. Your boating season is also effectively extended.

Many of today's advanced river techniques evolved from racing techniques. Competition speeds up the process of technical development; creativity flourishes when something's at stake. A classic example is the duffek stroke. The development and evolution of squirt boating can be traced back to slalom racing as well. Racers discovered that if slalom boats were lowered significantly in volume, they could be snuck under slalom poles, shortening the racer's path and saving time. It was then found that a boat with a low stern could be turned quickly with the help of a pivot turn. Squirt boating was born, and is now an area of kayaking that requires its own specific skills.

Slalom Rules

In a nutshell, the aim of whitewater slalom is to negotiate twenty-five gates cleanly without touching them with your body, boat, or paddle in the fastest possible time. Each gate is suspended from a wire across the river and consists of two poles which are never less than 1.2 meters (about 4 feet) from one another. The poles are hung 6 or more inches above the water's surface, allowing you to sneak at least some of your boat under them.

Gates are either red or green. Green gates are negotiated in a downstream direction (you come from upstream, go through the gate, and continue downstream) and are called downstream gates. Your boat may pass through a downstream gate facing forward, sideways, or backward. Red gates are negotiated from downstream to upstream. They're called upstream gates or ups and are usually placed in an eddy.

Any time you hit one or both poles of a gate, a penalty of 5 seconds is added to your total time. For each gate you miss, 50 seconds is added.

Gates have to be run sequentially. If you miss one, you're allowed to go back up for it provided you haven't yet negotiated any subsequent gates. This is called looping and adds a lot to your running time.

At a slalom race, you'll get at least one practice run and two timed and scored race runs. The overall race results are based on the score of the best of the two runs. The average raw time (without penalties) for a typical slalom course is 2½ to 3½ minutes.

STROKES TIMING. Initially, one of the most frustrating things about slalom is catching the pole with your paddle. When you do, it swings wildly and always seems to crash back at you like a manic boomerang. Per Murphy's Law, it always seems that the colder it is, the more it aims for your sensitive, ice-cold knuckles. To avoid this, learn to place your paddle in certain spots relative to the gate. Stroke timing will help you maximize your efficiency. For example, you can cure the problem of "chopping wood" by timing your strokes before and after the gate. This way, your paddle will be vertical as you actually go through the gate and the top blade won't smack or snare a pole.

As you approach a gate, you may need to adjust the length and power of some of your strokes in order to take the correct stroke before you go through the gate. You may have to do a partial stroke to maintain the correct cadence. Or you may have to do two consecutive strokes on the same side to put your boat in the right place, as well as to maintain the beat. Being able to automatically adjust your strokes to fit in the given space is an important skill to develop. For the most part, it's performed unconsciously. The more you are aware of it, however, the faster it'll come.

KNOWING THE COURSE. This may seem obvious, but besides using your best boating skills, remembering the course is the most important thing to do. On a race course you can cheat by reading the numbers on gates, but having to look up at every gate will distract you. You should be planning your line to a gate several gates in advance, and you can't do this very well if you're paddling by numbers. You want to get to the point where you know the gates and the water by heart so that you can focus exclusively on placing your strokes. Always plan your strategy sev-

Slalom Basics

eral gates in advance; if you take it a gate at a time, you'll eventually get so far off the line that you'll either miss a gate or lose a lot of time getting back on track. Anticipate. Don't let the water surprise you, though at times it will. Try to outfox it; let it do the work for you. The more you struggle, the more you fight the water. Racing should be strenuous because you push yourself to your physical limits, not because you do battle with the river as you run the course.

When looking at a slalom sequence, look closely at what the water is doing. The better you can anticipate, the quicker you can react. Consider the following factors, along with the location of the gates, when planning your route.

• Which way are various currents moving?
• How deep is the water?
• Where's the fastest, smoothest water?
• Are there rocks that can hit or snag your paddle?

Notice where slack water exists and avoid it if possible. If you can't, be ready for it so that it doesn't eddy you out or veer you off-line. Avoid shallow water, which will slow your boat. Above all, know what strokes you want to do and where to do them. You don't have to have every stroke memorized, but at least remember the important ones.

SMOOTH POWER. When you slalom race, it's important to be fast, not frantic. If you flail and splash water, you're probably wasting energy. Try to paddle hard but smoothly and efficiently. Paddle fast through an easy section of the course, but slow down for a difficult tight move. A fast time will come from precision more often than from raw speed. In slalom, there are times when it's fast to go fast and times when it's fast to go slow. Knowing when to adjust your speed is probably the most difficult, yet important, slalom skills.

Try to maintain your boat at an even speed. When you do need to accelerate and decelerate, do it smoothly. When accelerating, don't just hammer away. Do a few solid and strong strokes to get the boat up to speed.

Paddling increasingly harder can make you increasingly sloppy. You can paddle anaerobically all-out for only about 10 seconds, so you'll have to pace yourself. You want to be near the end of your strength when you cross the finish line. Also, because boats have a maximum hull speed built into their design, the increase in speed you get between 95 and 99 percent paddling effort is insignificant. Save your energy for when you really need it—at the end of the course or some place where there's a particularly tough sequence. It's not uncommon for a racer to take one run going all out and then to take the other at a seemingly slower, more conscientious pace. Often, the latter will in fact be the better run.

SNEAKING. Since the legal minimum pole height off the water is 6 inches, you'll often be able to sneak at least some of your bow and stern under one or both poles. The lower your boat, the more of it you can sneak. Sneaking allows you to avoid hitting poles and to save time by taking a shorter path.

In any kind of boat, but especially a low-volume racing boat, you can sneak your bow by doing a sweep stroke at the same time that you lean forward. But watch it: A sweep can raise your bow if your boat has too much forward momentum or is already turning that way. You can also do a powerful bow draw as you lean forward to sneak your bow. The faster and more you lean forward, the quicker and deeper your bow will bob down. If your boat is moving backward, try a reverse sweep as you snap your body forward. Be careful to synchronize your forward lunge with your stroke so that the boat goes down as it travels under the pole. If you time this incorrectly, the bow may sink down and then bob up to hit the pole. To sink your stern, do a sweep stroke with some forward momentum. Leaning back will push the stern down even more. Although there are many times when it's faster to sneak as much as you can, remember that the most important thing is to be well positioned for your next move. Depending on what's next, it might not be to your advantage to sneak a large proportion of your boat. The most important consideration is to keep the boat moving on the fastest, smoothest track.

Slalom Moves

Like river paddling, good slaloming depends on your technical skill, your ability to read white water, and your strategy. Strategy is determining where to put the boat before and after each gate. It's your angle and speed. It's figuring out where to really hammer down and where to slow up to ace the move. It's keeping in mind your own limits. The pace you choose must depend on your own endurance and strength as well as the length and difficulty of the course. Don't take the faster but riskier line if your present skill level dictates the conservative approach.

Now for some common whitewater slalom moves. Many slalom moves require you to use the water in ways that have already been described: ferries, surfs, and eddy turns, to name a few. The primary difference is that now there are gates and therefore you need to be more precise. The point of this chapter is to demonstrate a more analytical way of looking at white water. Even if you never get involved in slalom, your river-running skills will benefit from this approach. Being methodical, however, must not interfere with the fluidity and spontaneity of athletic movement. Things happen too fast on white water for you to think, "Okay, now I want to do a duffek . . ." If you can't make this instinctive, you'll suffer from that well-known affliction, Paralysis by Analysis.

DOWNSTREAMS IN WAVES. If it's a relatively straight line through two or more gates (rare in slalom), then just sprint through them. There are, however, a few tricks that will maximize your speed and efficiency, especially in waves. First of all, lean forward ever so slightly as you paddle. This keeps your bow from planing up, which will sink your stern and slow you. Adjust your body to your speed so that your boat's waterline is at its longest—the longer your waterline, the faster your hull speed. Also, try to take a forward stroke as your boat hits a wave. This will minimize the slowing caused by the impact. Try to place your forward stroke on a wave's downstream side. This makes it easier to pull your body through the wave. Avoid the wave peaks if the gate placements allow; the higher the part of the wave you go through or over, the more your boat speed decreases. Remember, it's much easier to turn at the peak of a wave when your ends are out of the water. If you have to turn, turn here.

OFFSETS. A series of three or more gates that are staggered are called offsets. Offset combinations can be easy or difficult. They can be some of the most deceiving gate sequences on the course. After all, what could be easier than paddling downstream while turning through gates? But beware, gates in an offset combination can really sneak up on you, especially in fast or surging water. Tight offsets can be so deceptive that one miscalculation or poorly placed stroke can cause you to *fifty*, or miss, one or more gates in the sequence.

The standard way of designating poles is this: the outside pole is the pole that is on your outside as you turn through a gate. For example, if you turn left while running a downstream gate, the right pole is the outside pole, and the other, the inside. If you were to travel through the gate turning to the other direction, the inside and outside poles would switch.

OFFSETS

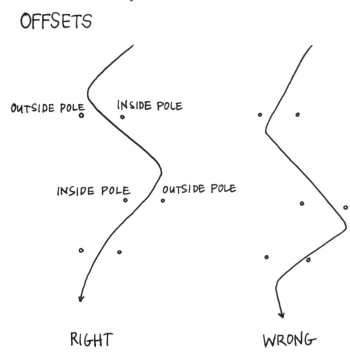

OUTSIDE POLE   INSIDE POLE

INSIDE POLE   OUTSIDE POLE

RIGHT   WRONG

Offsets. It's best to turn before each staggered gate. You'll increase your efficiency if you don't use drastic turning strokes. Instead, use subtle boat leans and forward strokes that contain minor turning components. Poles are designated according to whether they are to the inside or the outside of the paddler's turn.

Always turn as much as you can before and to the outside of the gate. This allows your boat a somewhat sideways orientation to the gate, giving you a good line to subsequent gates. In extreme cases, you can even come through the first gate with your bow pointed upstream and ferry over to the next gate. If you wait until after the gate to turn, chances are the next gate will come up awfully fast. Soon, you'll be scrambling for each gate—a slow and inefficient way to run a slalom.

The less offset the gates are, the more you'll want to maneuver through them using small draw–forward strokes and minimal stern draws. Keep them as small as possible; you don't want to turn too much and then have to correct.

If the gates are quite offset, use more powerful bow draws and sweeps to turn your boat. The tighter the sequence, the more you have to think ahead. Your bow draw should be placed a few feet above the gate so that

In severe offsets or in fast current, the direct line may not be feasible. A full-spin reverse or back ferry may be worth considering. The arrowheads show the direction of the bow.

ALTERNATIVE OFFSET STRATEGIES

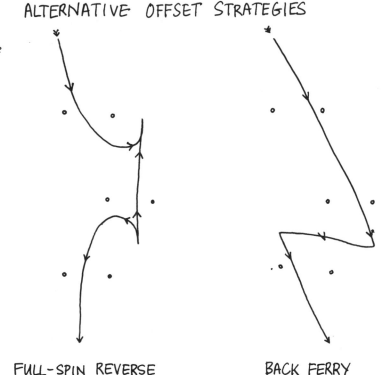

FULL-SPIN REVERSE   BACK FERRY

your snappy turn is done before you go through the gate. Turn a little to the outside of the gate so that you can gain some speed to get yourself to the next one.

Paradoxically, in profoundly offset gates, you have more options. If you're good, you can run them all directly. Or you can do one or more reverse, or back ferry between two of the gates.

Whenever you do duffeks and bow draws in offsets, try to do them as quickly as possible. The longer the blade is in the water, the more you'll slow the boat. But don't take the blade out prematurely. If it's still functional, use it while it's already there in the water. After you finish your duffek, go to a sweep or forward stroke on your downstream side as soon as you can reach through the gate. The faster you switch strokes, the less you'll get carried down the current between gates.

AN UPSTREAM GATE IN AN EDDY. An upstream gate is good if it's located in a well-defined eddy, if it's high in the eddy where the eddy is strongest, if it's close enough to the eddyline that you can exit back into the current with one stroke, and if it's deep enough in the eddyline that you can get into the meat of the eddy where your boat turns best.

To do an upstream gate well, you need to get a lot of crosscurrent momentum. Hit the eddyline at an angle between 60 and 80 degrees to the eddyline, if possible. Set yourself up so that your turn occurs about 4 feet downstream of the gate and slightly to the outside of the outside pole. This way, you'll give yourself the optimal exit angle, tight to the inside pole. Hit the eddy deep and low to the gate, but keep your speed up throughout to carve the turn. If the upstream gate is well-placed in the eddy, carving is faster and more efficient than wrapping closely around the inside pole, even though a good carve may take you on a longer line. It may seem like your boat is placed too low relative to the gate, but if you hit the eddy well, you'll fly right up through the gate in no time, often in only one or two strokes.

Switch to a quick exit stroke, either a forward stroke or a sweep on your upstream side. This stroke will launch you back into the current. It can be placed

IDEAL UPSTREAM

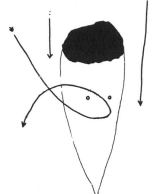

For this gate, it's best to hit the eddy low to the gate and to aim for the outside pole. Maintaining boat speed is crucial, even if it requires traveling a slightly longer path. Exit close to the inside pole if possible. When exiting an upstream gate, keep the next gate in mind so that you can adjust your exit angle accordingly.

either upstream or downstream of the line of the gate—usually upstream. If you do your exit stroke before the gate, be careful not to hit the gate with your paddle. Gauge your exit angle and the strength and type of exit stroke, always keeping in mind the location of the next gate. If the next gate is far downstream, you can peel directly out. If the next gate is crosscurrent, however, you'll need a ferry angle as you exit.

AN UPSTREAM IN CURRENT. This is the antithesis of an ideal upstream gate because you don't have an eddy to help you. If you can do this upstream well, you can do any "up" well. The upstream is usually set in slow-moving water or smack over the eddyline. To run it, come into the gate from the side and point upstream with a ferry angle. Sneak as much of your bow as you can under the inside pole. You don't want to be low in the gate and have to grunt your way upstream. If you can't ferry into the gate, you'll have to pull on a powerful duffek at the last moment—also lots of work, but your best bet.

With an upstream that's right over an eddyline, try to stay next to the pole nearest the eddy. It's easier to paddle up an eddy than against the current. Wherever the gate is placed, make sure you exit high enough. This will prevent you from hitting the inside pole as you peel out and continue to the next gate.

DOUBLE UPSTREAMS. A double upstream is two upstream gates hung on the same wire and separated by some current. Running it requires a move just like a current S turn, but with gates. It's best to come across perpendicular to the current, even if you end up hitting the second eddy low. If you hit this eddy with a good angle, perpendicular to the eddyline, you'll get a good carve in the eddy and be able to fly through the second upstream gate. This will be faster than pointing upstream and ferrying into the second up. There are a couple of exceptions. If the current is wide and fast, you may have to ferry most of the way, turning downstream just before you hit the eddyline to get the best approach. If the second up is in some current or on the eddyline, you'll have to make sure you have a ferry angle as you come high into the gate, just as you do with any upstream in current.

S TURNS. S turns are some of the fastest and slickest moves on a slalom course. Enter as parallel to the gate line as you can; aim to be about a foot or two below the inside pole. Plant your duffek as soon as you enter the eddy and adjust the blade angle to orient yourself correctly. You'll have to convert your duffek to a sweep or stern draw while you're in the gate, so be careful not to hit the poles. Change from a duffek to a stern draw right after your paddle crosses the gate line but before your body does. You want your sweep to come into force just as your body crosses the line. With a minimal S shape, you travel the fastest, most direct line. If you're really cutting it close, you'll probably have to slide your duffek to hip level before converting it into a stern draw. You may even have to sneak your forearm under the inside pole at your elbow.

When the gate is in a wide eddy, you have to paddle across the eddy before, after, or on both sides of the gate, depending on where the gate is. If you can negotiate the gate with a wide S shape done with forward strokes, you may not have to do a duffek.

Once again, always look to the next gate to gauge your exit angle. S-turn gates are so fast and fun that it's easy to get carried away and peel out too soon.

FULL-SPIN REVERSES. Although reverse gates aren't mandatory in the slalom world any more, it is strategically wise to know how to do one. A full-spin reverse is a 360-degree spin done as you negotiate a gate. You come in on one side from upstream and exit downstream of the gate, traveling back the way you came. You may want to do a gate backward to get the best setup for the next gate. There are two situations in which a full spin should be considered: from an upstream to a down on the same wire where the current is fast and there's a third downstream gate below the up, and in offset combinations where it's too tight or too risky to do the offset directly with a downstream boat orientation. The full spin tends to slow the boat down somewhat and can give you the angle and

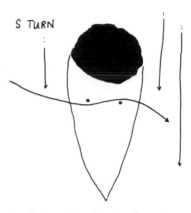

An S turn that cuts close to both poles will minimize traveling distance. The more the boat turns upstream in the eddy, the more it will stall. Convert the duffek to a stern draw between poles.

time you need to negotiate the next gate in the offset combination.

With a low-volume racing boat, the full spin is basically a pivot move. If you have a higher-volume boat, you can use the same stroke combination without sinking the stern, but you'll have to start your spin sooner, since you can't turn as quickly. Keep your bow low as you pivot. It may not look as impressive as a high pivot, but it's faster. Try to come in from the side as much as possible. How early you start your spin depends on the speed of the current; the faster the current, the earlier you'll want to initiate your spin. In general, start your reverse sweep just as your body is even and a few feet upstream of the inside pole. You may want a reverse stroke–sweep combination to push you through the gate.

Once you're through the gate, you can continue to spin the boat by turning your reverse sweep into a draw or by doing a forward sweep on the opposite side. The draw will be in position on the downstream side of your boat and can pull you crosscurrent if that's where the next gate is. Or, if you need to travel directly downstream, you can sweep on the upstream side, zipping the boat around and on downstream.

FERRY SEPARATED BY SLOW WATER. Anytime you ferry, you have to watch the water closely. If the current is consistent all the way across, you can just set your angle and paddle. Often, though, current is interspersed with eddies or relatively slack areas. The strength of these differentials dictates the degree to which you have to adjust your angle upstream or downstream as you ferry.

Don't let yourself get eddied out by slack water; you'll end up taking an undesirable circuitous route. To avoid this, angle your boat a bit downstream just before you hit the slower water. When the eddy catches you and turns your bow upstream you'll end up with the optimal ferry angle. The faster and broader your ferry is, the less the slow water will catch your boat.

TWO DOWNS SEPARATED BY AN EDDY. This move is basically an S turn, but it can occur with or without a distinct S shape, depending on where

DOWNS SEPARATED BY EDDY

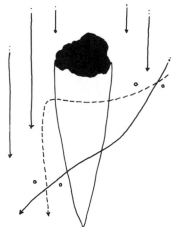

When negotiating two downstream gates separated by an eddy, it's usually quickest to take the path shown by the solid line. This takes the boat through very little slack eddy water. The dashed line is a possibility if you want a high margin of safety or if the third gate in this sequence were placed to river left of the second down.

the gates are located, the strength of the eddy, and your ability.

If the gates are both on the same wire, you have to turn upstream to get a good approach for the second gate. More often, the second gate is placed somewhat downstream relative to the first. When this is the case, paddle as low across the eddy as possible, where the eddy is weakest. This minimizes your boat's upstream turn. By going low, you stay in current longer than if you paddle across the eddy; this is fast and efficient. If your bow does start to turn upstream too much, place a quick sweep on your upstream side. Try placing a downstream duffek or a slight upstream stern draw. As you get more proficient, you'll be able to do this move with forward strokes and boat leans only. You won't need any correctional strokes. The faster you zip across an eddy, the less time there is for you to eddy out. To allow yourself plenty of room to negotiate, you can go through the first gate fairly sideways and do an S turn. This is slower, but depending on the placement of subsequent gates, it may be worth considering.

A DOWN IN AN EDDY OR ON AN EDDYLINE.

If the downstream gate is deep in the eddy, use the downstream-in-an-eddy technique (see Chapter Eight). Remember, the more you point downstream as you hit the eddy, the less the eddy will be able to eddy you out. Stay close to the inside pole to cut down on your traveling distance, as well as to avoid getting flung into the eddy.

If the gate is close to or on the eddyline and the next gate isn't far downstream, consider the *bogie*. To bogie the gate means that you go through the gate as flat (sideways) as you can and do a quick eddy turn on the far side. As you travel upstream in the eddy, you'll paddle above the gate you just negotiated and then ferry or paddle over for the next gate after you peel out. You end up traveling a greater distance, but if you do it effectively, it can be faster than muscling your way directly from gate to gate. How efficient a bogie is depends on the placement of the second gate. If it's close to the first or fairly downstream, try running the sequence directly, using forward strokes, duffeks, and sweeps. If the second gate is crosscurrent in fast water, the bogie may be your best bet.

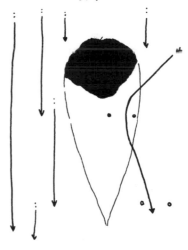

DOWN IN EDDY

To run this gate, come straight down on top of it as much as possible. Stay close to the inside pole to avoid the strongest part of the eddy.

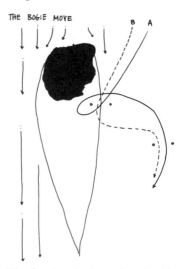

THE BOGIE MOVE

The bogie strategy (route A) requires the boater to travel farther than route B does. But the eddy gives the turn a boost and allows for such a good approach to the next gate that the extra distance pays off.

At the Races

You may think that the more practice you can get on the course, the better your run will be. To some extent this is true, but just running the course 100 times won't help much if you don't understand the aquatic nuances. Before you run the course take some time to memorize it and plan your strategy from the shore. Select your primary routes, but also have alternative paths. Watching other boaters paddle the course helps. Are they consistently getting caught off guard by some invisible current and flying past a gate? How can you avoid making the same mistake?

As you walk the course, check it out from various perspectives. You'll probably notice new angles to things. Examine the course from both sides of the river; some gates might be too far from one bank for you to see important details well.

VISUALIZING THE COURSE. After scouting from shore, mentally go back through the course, remembering as many details about the water and the gates as you can. Visualize the course until you can make it all the way down without forgetting a detail. Once you have the course memorized, you can take a run without stopping every few gates to regain your bearings.

At some smaller races you're allowed as many practice runs as you want, but at bigger races one practice run is standard. If you're allowed more than one, take your first run at a slow pace. This will give you time to think about which aspects of your strategy are working and which ones need to be adjusted. It's natural for things to be different on the water than you figured from shore. Don't be shy about asking other boaters their opinions of certain sequences. They're always a good source of information.

RACING. After your practice runs and before the race runs, look for changes in the course. Check to see if the water level has changed or whether any poles have sagged low to the water. It might be best to run the first few gates solidly, but not at an all out pace. Getting off to a good start helps prevent you from making early panic-induced blunders, and you'll be able to set a good pace. Once you're going, increase your speed to whatever feels right. Nervousness usually disappears as soon as you start down the course.

If you have a good first run, give it your all on your second. If you have a poor first run, recognize your mistakes and try to correct them. Don't be too hard on yourself. You'll be that much more experienced for the second run. Watch other boaters between your runs to gather additional information.

START AND FINISH STRATEGIES. If you're starting near the bank in shallow water, consider poling off a rock to get a solid start. You may have the option of paddling through slack water to get to the first gate or taking a longer line that has deeper water. Consider the trade-offs; the longer path may be faster overall if it puts you in the current sooner.

There are a few things to consider when you're going for the finish line. First, see whether the finish line is angled across the river. If one side is upstream of the other and all other factors are equal, that will be the side to aim for. Also check where the fastest, deepest current crosses the finish; if other things are equal, go there.

As you negotiate the course and approach the last gates, put every ounce of strength into your strokes. The end is near.

Suggested Reading and Viewing

BOOKS

Bechdel, Les and Slim Ray. *River Rescue*. Appalachian Mountain Club Books, Boston: 1985.

Endicott, William. *The Ultimate Run*. 6537 Broad St., Bethesda, MD 20816.

Evans, Eric and Jay Evans. *The Kayaking Book*. The Stephen Greene Press, Lexington, Massachusetts: 1988.

Nealy, William. *Kayak*. Menasha Ridge Press, Birmingham, Alabama: 1986.

Snyder, James. *The Squirt Book*. Menasha Ridge Press, Birmingham, Alabama: 1987.

Tejada-Flores, Lito. *Wildwater: Sierra Club Guide to Kayaking and Whitewater Boating*. Sierra Club Books, San Francisco: 1978.

VIDEOS

"Kayak Playpaddling with Bob McDougall." Gravity Sports Films, Inc., 100 Broadway, Jersey City, NJ 07306.

"Fast and Clean." Gravity Sports Films, Inc., 100 Broadway, Jersey City, NJ 07306.